# THE WASTE LAND

TS Eliot

9

Editors:
Linda Cookson
Bryan Loughrey

LONGMAN
LITERATURE
GUIDES

## Longman Literature Guides

Editors: Linda Cookson and Bryan Loughrey

Titles in the series:

# CONTENTS

## A practical guide to essay writing 137

## Suggestions for further reading 155

# PREFACE

Like all professional groups, literary critics have developed their own specialised language. This is not necessarily a bad thing. Sometimes complex concepts can only be described in a terminology far removed from everyday speech. Academic jargon, however, creates an unnecessary barrier between the critic and the intelligent but less practised reader.

This danger is particularly acute where scholarly books and articles are re-packaged for a student audience. Critical anthologies, for example, often contain extracts from longer studies originally written for specialists. Deprived of their original context, these passages can puzzle and at times mislead. The essays in this volume, however, are all specially commissioned, self-contained works, written with the needs of students firmly in mind.

This is not to say that the contributors — all experienced critics and teachers — have in any way attempted to simplify the complexity of the issues with which they deal. On the contrary, they explore the central problems of the text from a variety of critical perspectives, reaching conclusions which are challenging and at times mutually contradictory.

They try, however, to present their arguments in a direct, accessible language and to work within the limitations of scope and length which students inevitably face. For this reason, essays are generally rather briefer than is the practice; they address quite specific topics; and, in line with examination requirements, they incorporate precise textual detail into the body of the discussion.

They offer, therefore, working examples of the kind of essay-writing skills which students themselves are expected to develop. Their diversity, however, should act as a reminder that in the field of literary studies there is no such thing as a 'model' answer. Good essays are the outcome of a creative engagement with literature, of sensitive, attentive reading and careful thought. We hope that those contained in this volume will encourage students to return to the most important starting point of all, the text itself, with renewed excitement and the determination to explore more fully their own critical responses.

# How to use this volume

Obviously enough, you should start by reading the text in question. The one assumption that all the contributors make is that you are already familiar with this. It would be helpful, of course, to have read further — perhaps other works by the same author or by influential contemporaries. But we don't assume that you have yet had the opportunity to do this and any references to historical background or to other works of literature are explained.

You should, perhaps, have a few things to hand. It is always a good idea to keep a copy of the text nearby when reading critical studies. You will almost certainly want to consult it when checking the context of quotations or pausing to consider the validity of the critic's interpretation. You should also try to have access to a good dictionary, and ideally a copy of a dictionary of literary terms as well. The contributors have tried to avoid jargon and to express themselves clearly and directly. But inevitably there will be occasional words or phrases with which you are unfamiliar. Finally, we would encourage you to make notes, summarising not just the argument of each essay but also your own responses to what you have read. So keep a pencil and notebook at the ready.

Suitably equipped, the best thing to do is simply begin with whichever topic most interests you. We have deliberately organised each volume so that the essays may be read in any order. One consequence of this is that, for the sake of clarity and self-containment, there is occasionally a degree of overlap between essays. But at least you are not forced to follow one — fairly arbitrary — reading sequence.

Each essay is followed by brief 'Afterthoughts', designed to highlight points of critical interest. But remember, these are only there to remind you that it is *your* responsibility to question what you read. The essays printed here are not a series of 'model' answers to be slavishly imitated and in no way should they be regarded as anything other than a guide or stimulus for your own thinking. We hope for a critically involved response: 'That was interesting. But if *I* were tackling the topic . . .!'

Read the essays in this spirit and you'll pick up many of the skills of critical composition in the process. We have, however, tried to provide more explicit advice in 'A practical guide to essay writing'. You may find this helpful, but do not imagine it offers any magic formulas. The quality of your essays ultimately depends on the quality of your engagement with literary texts. We hope this volume spurs you on to read these with greater understanding and to explore your responses in greater depth.

**Pat Pinsent**

*Pat Pinsent is Principal Lecturer in English at the Roehampton Institute of Higher Education.*

ESSAY

# 'Genuine poetry can communicate before it is understood.'[1] Is this true of *The Waste Land?*

Critical guides to *The Waste Land* invariably devote much of their attention to interpretation of the poem, tracing some of its sources, translating the many quotations from esoteric writers, relating it to Eliot's biography and to the history of Europe. This process is inevitable and much of it is probably essential. Yet there is the danger that once this process is (relatively) complete, and the reader of the criticism has (almost) understood the explication, too little space will be left for appreciation of the poem as poetry. This is of course always a danger; students often complain of 'pulling a poem to pieces', neglecting the essential process of putting it together again after the significance of the different aspects has been understood.

---

[1] T S Eliot, 'Essay on Dante', in *Collected Prose* (London, 1975).

This danger is perhaps particularly acute in the case of *The Waste Land* because of the quantity and complexity of the explanations needed before it can to any real extent be understood. Eliot himself intensified this effect by his provision of Notes, so that once students have followed up his references to Weston's *From Ritual to Romance* and Frazer's *The Golden Bough*, they feel they have 'mastered' the poem. The process is felt to be complete at the point where 'reading' the poem as a work of literature ought to be starting.

My intention in this essay is to work the other way round, to assume no more background knowledge than the reasonably well-read student of *English* literature would bring with her to the reading of the poem, and to examine how far the poem itself can communicate. As Eliot says in his 'Essay on Dante', a poet he enjoyed in spite of his inadequate knowledge of Italian:

> It is better to be spurred to acquire scholarship because you enjoy the poetry, than to suppose that you enjoy the poetry because you have acquired the scholarship.

I suspect that many readers have treated *The Waste Land* like a superior form of crossword puzzle, and have 'enjoyed' the poem only in so far as they have been able to respond to all the 'clues', including those in the Notes supplied by the poet. It is my contention that there is much in the poem to which the intelligent reader can immediately respond, using no more than the sensitivity to word, sound and image which should have developed naturally in any serious student of English. Through this response, a real apprehension of part of the poet's meaning should be achieved, and, hopefully, this should motivate the reader to 'acquire scholarship'.

I propose therefore to give a good deal of close attention to 'The Burial of the Dead', and rather less, because of space constraints, to the rest of the work. I want to show how the reader begins to work towards a tentative construct of meaning, to be verified by further study, motivated in turn by curiosity: 'What did he *really* mean?'

Without an initial interest in any work of literature, the reader who is not forced into reading by the constraints of examinations will not proceed far! The durability of *The*

*Waste Land* over the last sixty-five years suggests that it had qualities which hold and intrigue, ensuring perseverance past the initial puzzlement. A fresh glance at the opening lines supports this:

> *I   The Burial of the Dead*
> April is the cruellest month, breeding
> Lilacs out of the dead land, mixing
> Memory and desire, stirring
> Dull roots with spring rain.

We are immediately aware of the juxtaposition of contrasting elements: the negative associations of the titles, both of the whole work and of this section, and of words such as 'dead' and 'dull' constrast with the affirmative qualities of 'April', 'lilacs' and 'spring'. The almost paradoxical 'cruellest' is perhaps the focus here; it intrigues us as the first sentence of a novel might, making us want to read on and discover why April, traditionally associated with sweet showers and joy, is cruel. We are also led on syntactically by the abundance of present participles which end five of the first seven lines, thus creating a sensation of movement which is reinforced throughout the first eighteen lines. The language is very economical; paradoxically and alliteratively 'Winter kept us warm' (1.5). Unexpectedly yet aptly 'snow' is described as 'forgetful' (does the snow forget to thaw or is the epithet transferred, the snow making *us* forget what it hides?). Summer is personified: it 'surprised us' as a friend's sudden arrival might.

Our involvement is aided by the poet's use of the first person plural; we are drawn in because he tells us that 'we' are there and it would seem almost rude to contradict him or to say that we don't understand or share the experience he describes. Even if we are ignorant of both the geographical position of the 'Starnbergersee' or the 'Hofgarten' and the meaning of line 12: 'Bin gar keine Russin, stamm' aus Litauen, echt Deutsch', the effective verbal pictures create empathy. The action seems to oscillate between present and past, and the poet evokes in his reader senses other than the visual: the babble of voices, the perfume of the lilacs, the taste of the coffee, and the sensation of tobogganing down the mountains:

> . . . he took me out on a sled,
> And I was frightened. He said, Marie,
> Marie, hold on tight. And down we went.

(ll.14–16)

These effects are reinforced by the subtle use of sound, such as the monosyllables of line 4, the sibilant 's' with an occasional liquid 'l' in lines 8 to 10:

> Summer surprised us, coming over the Starnbergersee
> With a shower of rain; we stopped in the colonnade,
> And went on in sunlight . . .

The slower final line (l.18) 'I read much of the night, and go south in winter' creates a distancing effect after the movement of much of this sub-section, so that by the end of this opening verse paragraph, we have not only been given a sense of pleasing anticipation of what is to follow but have also gained an implicit awareness of many of the themes of the poem: past and present, a fragmented Europe, death and rebirth.

The next few lines may well engender surprise, even anxiety. Where is the voice of 'Marie'? Surely not in this authoritative, even biblical ('Son of man') and somewhat threatening tone? This very insecurity chimes in with the poet's purpose and reinforces the contrast between the almost lush beginning of the poem and the desert here which makes us immediately more aware of the poem's title — more emphatically I would suggest, in spite of the absence of narrative order, than if Eliot had begun with this section. After the relative economy of words and the fast movement we have experienced, we are beset by repetition, given a longer line which at first lulls us into an expectation of the iambic as it departs from the speech rhythms we have just experienced, but which becomes irregular in beat as it presents to us the catalogue of 'broken images'. Having been brought so organically into the poem at its beginning, it is our own 'shadow' we see, it is our own 'fear in a handful of dust'. Even if the echoes of Ezekiel and the metaphysical poets do not awaken any response in us, the patterning created by the sounds of the clutching 'roots', the 'stony rubbish', the 'red rock' and the repeated 'shadow', the now 'threatening' sun and the reversion to the present participles given by 'striding' and 'rising', all engender the expectation of a kind of horror, reinforced by the absence of any life other than that largely negated in line 23, with the 'dead tree'. Again, we may be left with many questions, but the poetry has communicated.

The insertion of further German lines can be more puzzling:

> *Frisch weht der Wind*
> *Der Heimat zu*
> *Mein Irisch Kind,*
> *Wo weilest du?*

(ll.31–34)

> *Oed' und leer das Meer.*

(l.42)

No translation is provided; Eliot merely refers us to Wagner's opera *Tristan and Isolde*, so that this can make still more acute the question of whether poetry can communicate before it is understood. The reader unfamiliar with German will have to rely on the sound of the words (probably inaccurately pronounced) and will perhaps guess those words nearest the English ('*Wind*', '*Irisch*' and '*Kind*'?) What can the lines convey? The sense that the poem is about Europe is reinforced; the wind relates to natural elements of water, sun and dust already mentioned. If an attempt is made to read the words aloud, the rhyme (so far absent in the poem) and the shorter lines also have an effect. The first four lines act as a bridge to the 'hyacinth girl' lines which follow, and are contained by the final German line. The one word for which I think that translation is necessary for appreciation is '*Meer*'; without an understanding of the reference to the sea, some of the cohesion both of the subsection and of section I as a whole is lost, especially the link with the 'drowned Phoenician Sailor' (l.47) of the 'clairvoyante' passage which follows. Overall, the contrast between the desert of lines 19 and 30 and the lushness of the hyacinth garden of lines 35 to 41 is intensified by the unfamiliar language. Certainly the latter section, with the sensual impact of 'Your arms full, and your hair wet' linking with the perfumed fleshy flower, enhances the overall dramatic effect. Is this yet another speaker, or Marie again? It cannot be the voice of lines 19 to 30, nor indeed that of the next part, but I question whether this issue detracts at all from the enjoyment of the poem by the reader who is content to let the words speak for themselves.

The next part sets us immediately in a different world, that of society where the current fashion is to consult 'Madame Sosostris, famous clairvoyante / . . . the wisest woman in Europe, / With a wicked pack of cards.' (ll.43–46). Perhaps her clients imagine they will be a little more in control of their fate when she consults the Tarot pack, here consorting incongruously with the everyday clichés of 'has a bad cold' (1.44) and 'One must be so careful these days' (1.59). The counterpointing effect of references such as 'the Lady of the Rocks' (1.48), both reminding us of the desert section and looking forward to later themes in the whole poem, is very characteristic of Eliot.

It is not until we have read the conclusion of this first movement of the poem that we attain the more complete aesthetic experience which I would claim is necessary for the poet to communicate to us. Its total meaning must of course be unattainable because Eliot's allusive method often embraces meanings peculiar to the poet's own experience, but we as readers do have access to a sufficiency of meaning to motivate us to find out more, to look into the sources, and in the first instance actually want to go on and read the remainder of the poem, preserving a state of expectation. With the concluding part, we find ourselves not in the desert, not in the hyacinth garden or the sophisticated drawing room, but in a city which is both London and the world. We have already met enough characters (even if we are far from sure how many) to believe in the crowd which 'flowed over London Bridge' (cutting transversely the flow of the river under the bridge). We are ourselves involved in this flow of humanity towards death; the picture is vivid, enhanced by Eliot's use of sound, especially in line 68: 'With a dead sound on the final stroke of nine.' We scarcely need to be told of Eliot's own experience in the city of London in order to share his feeling; being part of the collective isolation of rush hour in any city is enough to make us appreciate the way all the individuals are alone with their own fates. Here again we have a new tone, presumably that of a new speaker, indicated by the reversion to the longer line and the slightly more literary phrasing of 'undone so many' (1.63), 'exhaled' (1.64) and 'kept the hours' (1.67), which help us to go from the immediacy of twentieth-century London to the universality of death. That this includes us too is made apparent by the last few lines. We may not be directly addressed as 'Stetson' (1.69) but the use of the second person, 'You', includes us, even while we are puzzled and perturbed at the grotesque idea of a sprouting corpse. The 'tubers' of line 7 and the 'hyacinths' recur to our memories, the 'breeding' which April gives rise to can perhaps at last be seen as cruel, and even a meagre knowledge of French ensures that we find ourselves, as readers, addressed in the final line.

A reading such as that outlined obviously omits a good deal to which even someone relatively unpractised would respond, often at an implicit level, and which would create certain kinds of feeling and expectation to be taken into the rest of the poem. With all its inadequacies, however, I trust that it makes apparent the ways in which Eliot's themes, which he amplifies in the rest of the poem, can be glimpsed by means of an encounter with the poetic effects of his varied and evocative verse.

While it is clearly impossible for me to discuss the remainder of the poem in the same detail, briefer scrutiny may well serve to pinpoint a few instances where our hypothetical reader may well respond to the poetry, which communicates directly with her, before she makes the effort to understand in any depth. Passing regretfully 'A Game at Chess' with its richly derivative first section contrasted with the colloquial pub scene, and perhaps less regretfully 'the young man carbuncular' of 'The Fire Sermon', I shall focus firstly on 'Death by Water' and then on the challenge to my whole approach made by the final, particularly allusive, lines of the whole poem (ll.423–433).

Even the least experienced reader will, I am sure, link section IV, 'Death by Water', with Madame Sosostris's words, 'Here. . ./ is your card, the drowned Phoenician Sailor' (ll.46–47). This provides a means of unity not unlike that of music, where a theme suggested in the first movement of a symphony may well be taken up and treated differently in a later movement; such a mode of relating themes has always seemed to me helpful in reading Eliot's longer poems. Other than this, I would suggest that IV is best read as a unit, a brief epitaph which, in spite of our ignorance of the man who is its subject, manages to convey feeling, particularly through its final line, '. . . who was once handsome and tall as you.' We combine the regret for the dead man, presumably drowned in his prime, with a reminder of our own mortality; if he was once as we are, inevitably we shall become what he now is. The use of echoic expressions, such as 'the cry of gulls and the deep sea swell' (l.313) and 'A current under sea/ Picked his bones in whispers' (ll.315–316) almost imperceptibly enhances the effect of the lines; the poet's use of assonance in the vowels predisposes us to accept the meaning. The movement of the body of the dead man, 'As he rose and fell' (l.316) is deceptively active 'entering the whirlpool' (l.318), a movement supported by the rather inconspicuous use of rhyme in this part of the poem. The all-embracing command at the end, 'Consider . . .' (l.321) strikes just the right note of restraint so that the very absence of stated emotion makes these lines both personal and universal.

In reading section V, 'What the Thunder said', I feel that, for once, the poet's Notes do provide some help, in directing us to the resurrection narrative of the journey to Emmaus (Luke 24), as well as to the break-up of Eastern Europe. If this biblical and historical knowledge is seen as integral to the appreciation of the poem, an argument could be mounted that more direct reference within the text would have been preferable; to this issue I shall return. These early sections, then, provide the context for the final lines which I now propose to scrutinise, referring here again to the Notes. These direct us, for line 424, to the figure of the Fisher King:

> I sat upon the shore
> Fishing, with the arid plain behind me
> Shall I at least set my lands in order?
> London Bridge is falling down falling down falling down
>
> (ll.423–426)

I would contend that at the surface level we need no further knowledge of the background material in order to appreciate this reference than the very title of the poem, alluded to in 'the arid plain'. Dryness and water have been dominating images throughout, and we are clearly looking for a way for fertility to be restored to the land, through the agency of the king. Themes occurring elsewhere proliferate; 'London Bridge' takes us back to the procession of the dead in section I, linked this time with the falling towers of line 373, but perhaps made less threatening by its echo of the nursery song. The snatch from Dante's *Purgatorio*:

> *Poi s'ascose nel foco che gli affina*
> *Quando fiam uti chelidon.*
>
> (ll.427–428)

must, at the level at which I am discussing the poem, remain untranslated, for Eliot provides no more than its source in his Notes. This in itself can be useful, however, for it introduces the idea of hope for a fire that is purifying, a means to bliss, rather than the purely destructive element which the reference to 'Falling towers' (l.373) might have otherwise implied. The Italian, and the shorter English and French quotations which follow, certainly succeed in generating a sense of chaos:

> . . . O swallow swallow
> *Le Prince d'Aquitaine à la tour abolie.*
>
> (ll.428–429)

Line 430, however, 'These fragments have I shored against my ruins', evocative of the scene in a city once war is over and reconstruction can ensue, seems to me to provide, even for the naïve reader who has responded only to what she can accept without 'scholarship', at once a key to the poem and a hope of regeneration. Whether or not she is familiar with Kyd's *Spanish Tragedy*, alluded to in line 431, 'Why then Ile fit you. Hieronymo's mad againe', seems to me at this point to make little difference, for whatever the meaning to the poet, the lines here display how fragile any moment of sanity must be, how precarious the balance of the ruins. The poet does helpfully translate lines 432 ('Datta. Dayadhvam. Damyata', repeated from earlier in this Movement, where it has been revealed that what the thunder is saying is 'Give. Sympathise. Control') and 433, rendered by Eliot as 'The Peace which passeth understanding'. Thus, even for the reader who is doing no more than responding to the poem with the aid, where relevant, of Eliot's Notes, a satisfying conclusion is put on the experience, a means of unifying the fragments, of bringing renewal to the arid land, of revivifying the waste land. I would argue that this experience, while not wholly satisfying, has enough within it to cause such a reader to 'be spurred to acquire scholarship' in order to improve the reading.

Such a reader may, however, be left with a certain sense of disquiet. How much has been missed by not following up the more arcane references, notably those to Weston's book? How far would the experience of the poem have been still more incomplete without occasional use of the Notes (added, as we know, almost as an afterthought)? How valid can any aesthetic experience be which demands the reader to go outside of it for completeness? I would approach these questions on two fronts. Firstly, I think a case can be made for Eliot's use of esoteric sources which were resonant to him, and which certainly express his meaning, in the last few lines, more economically and more mellifluously than their translation could have done. Once they are understood, the further readings of the poem are enriched by them, and a simple substitution of the English words seems less satisfying. The very sound of the thrice repeated 'Shantih' is surely effective even when first encountered. Secondly, while claiming the validity of the experience of a naïve reading, I would recognise that there can never in fact be such a thing. A pure reading of any poem is impossible; we all bring with us associations from the world outside the poem, and these will not normally be the ones the poet has. Eliot may, as here, seek to provide a frame of reference against which to read a work of literature but even if we emulated his width of reading and made ourselves familiar with his personal experience, we could never read precisely the poem he wrote, any more than we can read poems which are apparently simpler by, for instance, Wordsworth or Tennyson. Given that the poem can never be fully 'understood', that, even to the most scholarly reader the communication must always be in some way partial, then I would claim that an untutored reading which responds to the poetry but fails to 'translate' or interpret the poem, has the advantage over a reading which is fully conversant with the sources and allusions but sees the poem as an exercise and does not succeed in 'putting it together again'. It is of course to be hoped that the reader who starts by appreciating the poetry without much knowledge will be motivated to acquire it. I am tempted to apply to Eliot's own work what he says of Dante's:

> There is an immense amount of knowledge which, until one has read some of his poetry with intense pleasure — that is, with as keen pleasure as one is capable of getting from any poetry — is positively undesirable.
>
> ('Essay on Dante')

That *The Waste Land* is genuine poetry which 'can communicate before it is understood' seems to me beyond question.

# AFTERTHOUGHTS

## 1

Pinsent quotes from Eliot's own 'Essay on Dante'. How helpful is it to know a writer's views on other authors?

## 2

Can the *sound* of language really communicate in the way that Pinsent suggests?

## 3

Eliot was a poet and critic. How much significance should we attach to his critical views when considering his poetry?

## 4

Do you agree that 'A pure reading of any poem is impossible' (page 18)?

**Tony Pinkney**

*Tony Pinkney teaches at Wadham College, Oxford. He is the author of* Women in the Poetry of T. S. Eliot: A Psychoanalytic Approach *(London, 1984), and has published articles on Eliot in various critical journals.*

## ESSAY

# The aristocracy in
# *The Waste Land*

*The Waste Land* is now an old poem: first published in 1922, it reached pension age in 1987. Claims that it expresses 'the spiritual crisis of modern man', 'the sterility of the modern experience', founder on the fact that it belongs to the youth of our great-grandfathers and grandmothers. Are *they* still 'modern', is their experience ours, has nothing changed in the intervening sixty-odd years? *The Waste Land* is a modern*ist* — not a modern and still less a contemporary — poem. It belongs, that is to say, to the great epoch of artistic experiment which spans the years from, say, 1890 to 1930. Modernism itself is now an old movement, although many English literary critics still offer Joyce, Yeats, Lawrence, Woolf and Eliot as speaking directly to 'us', to 'our' modernity. Rather than brusquely dragging *The Waste Land* into our own present, we ought, I suggest, to situate this frail and elderly text in its *own* historical moment, attending with due respect to what it can tell us about that.

The poem, it is generally agreed, is about crisis, dislocation, fragmentation, chaos. But just whose crisis does it evoke or enact? Once again, the temptation is to answer with that bland but rather unmeaning phrase, 'modern man'. It is to *The Waste Land*'s credit, however, that it gives us a more precise analysis than that. True, its opening lines are of great generality. They read as straightforward, even confident propositions. The spiritual pain they assert seems to admit of no qualification or exact location, and we may well be inclined to take the 'us' of 'Winter kept us warm' as alluding to a modern Everyman. But no sooner have we done so than the poem asks us to think again:

> Summer surprised us, coming over the Starnbergersee
> With a shower of rain; we stopped in the colonnade,
> And went on in sunlight, into the Hofgarten,
> And drank coffee, and talked for an hour.
> Bin gar keine Russin, stamm' aus Litauen, echt deutsch.
>
> (ll.8–12)

The reader is as surprised by Marie's lively intrusion into the poem's abstract solemnities as she is by the summer rain shower. What, then, is the relation between her 'us', the 'us' that summer surprises, and the 'us' whose little life is kept warm on a diet of dried tubers. The proponents of 'modern man' readings of *The Waste Land* see her as a mere exemplary instance of contemporary spiritual dessication. In this interpretation, Marie is interchangeable with a dozen other characters: at this point the poem might equally well have offered us Mrs Equitone, Stetson, Lil and Albert or the house agent's clerk, but it happens upon Marie, and so here she is. Once again, though, the poem has been drained of its specificity. We bleed it dry of historical precision by reading it as a discourse on an abstract 'modernity', and we drain Marie of her *individual* difference by treating her as a mere cipher for the subjective uncertainties of the 'modern age'. My own reading of the poem is rather different: I believe that her specific social identity as an Austrian aristocrat is at the very heart of the crisis that *The Waste Land* records. Her 'we' is not a local instance of the general 'we' of 'Winter kept us warm'; the opening 'we', rather, articulates the experience of Marie and her own class and has *no* further general validity. It is, as I hope to show, the aristocracy that is in crisis, not modern man.

Later in the poem the Fisher King fishes in the dull canal:

> Musing upon the king my brother's wreck
> And on the king my father's death before him.
>
> (ll.191–192)

22

He has good cause to be so doleful. For the five years preceding *The Waste Land*'s publication had been disastrous for traditional monarchies and aristocracies. The king my brother had been wrecked first in Russia, when the Bolshevik Revolution overthrew the Tsarist regime in 1917, then in Austro-Hungary, where the Habsburg Empire collapsed after the First World War, and finally in Germany, where Kaiser Wilhelm II was driven out by the revolution of 1918 (in turn followed by socialist insurrections in 1919). Eliot evokes these great social upheavals in 'What the Thunder said', though — diehard conservative that he was — he can see in them nothing more than anarchy, bloodbaths and the probable end of 'civilisation':

> Who are those hooded hordes swarming
> Over endless plains, stumbling in cracked earth
> Ringed by the flat horizon only
> What is that city over the mountains
> Cracks and reforms and bursts in the violet air
> Falling towers

(ll.368–373)

In the notes to these lines Eliot cites a passage from Hesse's *Blick ins Chaos* which discusses the probable consequences of the Russian Revolution. What Eliot here quaintly terms 'the present decay of Eastern Europe' was, in point of fact, a partial emancipation of whole peoples from extraordinarily repressive — and usually aristocratic — ruling classes.

If cities are cracking, reforming and bursting, we can begin to see why the first city to feature in the poem should be Munich, with its Starnbergersee and Hofgarten, and why, more generally, German voices and cultural allusions should so dominate the opening paragraphs of the poem. For Munich was one of the storm-centres of post-war revolution and counter-revolution. The King of Bavaria was ousted in late 1918; a socialist government led by Kurt Eisner was then set up in Munich, but Eisner was assassinated by a nationalist aristocrat (one of Marie's peers? the arch-duke her cousin?) in February 1919; the soviet-style workers' councils took over, driving out the socialists, and the Communists then assumed command; they were brutally put down by the army in May. Even more ominously, the young Austrian Adolf Hitler arrived in the city in April 1919, and proceeded to consolidate an extreme right-wing power-base. The Nazi Party was constituted in 1920, and in 1923 Hitler attempted a coup in Munich (he was, for the moment, unsuccessful and thrown in jail). Eliot had visited Munich in August 1911, and was later involved in work on the pre-war German debt for Lloyd's bank. The fact that, at the very start of *The Waste Land*, he so firmly locates the contemporary crisis in this particular German city shows how sensitive, even clairvoyant, he was to the currents of the post-war political situation.

Marie's status within her society is edgy and ambivalent. On the one hand, she seems to enjoy the routines of a wealthy, leisured and cultured existence, strolling about the Hofgarten, chatting for an hour over coffee, going south in the winter. Yet she also seems anxious and defensive. Her first spoken words respond, whether in anger or desperation, to some implicit racial or nationalist accusation: 'Bin gar keine Russin . . . echt deutsch' (l.12). Though she belongs to the very highest echelons of the Austrian aristocracy, with an arch-duke for cousin, her thoughts and memories are tinged with fear. Even innocent childhood phrases take on sinister political overtones in the context of that post-war future which young Marie and the arch-duke must face as adults. 'Hold on tight', he tells her (l.16), and the aristocracy had urgent need to do so from 1917 onwards. 'Down we went', she glumly reports, as the aristocracies of Russia, Austro-Hungary and Germany indeed did in those turbulent years. 'In the mountains, there you feel free' (l.17). The implication is that everywhere else you feel claustrophobic, threatened. The trip to the mountains may be either a temporary escape from the violent revolutionary ferment of cities like Munich, or the actual political exile that would overtake so many post-war aristocrats.

The post-war revolutions were made by demobilised soldiers, a fact which provides the social context for the second half of 'A Game of Chess': 'When Lil's husband got demobbed, I said —' (l.139). Albert does indeed seem to be in the grip of an explosive discontent, since 'He's been in the army four years, he wants a good time' (l.148). True, the satisfaction he seeks is sexual rather than political, and the atmosphere of this episode is one of broad, music-hall comedy rather than imminent danger. None the less, its social implications are brought out by the juxtaposition of this low-life scene with the weird, neurasthenic royal couple of the first half of this section. The Victorian poet and critic Matthew Arnold (who was a major influence on Eliot) once wrote that England was fortunate in having the most popular aristocracy and the most aristocratic people of all nations. The point of 'A Game of Chess' is to show how disastrously this desirable social unity has broken down. Only a faint memory of it survives, as when in 'The Fire Sermon' the third Thames-maiden recalls 'My people humble people who except/ Nothing' (ll.304–305). Such traditional deference no longer restrains Lil, Albert, Bill and May, just as, in 'The Fire Sermon', the typist and house agent's clerk, far from respecting Tiresias's classical authority, impudently proceed to copulate in front of him. It is the brash figure of Sweeney who, both here and elsewhere in Eliot's work, best embodies this anxiety about the crumbling of the social hierarchies which once held the populace in check. At any rate the 'royal' pair, whose situation opens 'A Game of Chess', certainly cannot provide social leadership. Incapable of even the most elementary gestures of political self-defence, they wait grimly for their own demise 'in rats' alley/Where the dead men lost their bones' (ll.115–116). Marie's childhood alarms have become much sharper in an epoch when, as in 'What the Thunder said', both 'Prison and palace' (l.326) are under threat: 'What is that noise? . . . What is that noise now?' (ll.117/119). The 'king' listlessly mimes the everyday routines of a secure aristocracy, but waits secretly and stoically for a revolutionary 'knock upon the door' (l.138). Marie still had places of refuge to turn to, but now even among the mountains, as we learn in 'What the Thunder said', 'red sullen faces sneer and snarl/ From doors of mudcracked houses' (ll.344–345).

How might this crisis of the aristocracy be overcome? One possible answer might be Tiresias, on whose success the poem stakes so much; he is, the notes tell us, 'the most important personage in the poem, uniting all the rest'. He thus projects the image of a unitary social consensus which no longer exists in contemporary history. He lays claim to a vision of totality, encompassing narrow, partial viewpoints; he has, precisely, foresuffered *all*. Tiresias is, we might say, *dis*interested rather than 'interested', as are all the other characters in the poem, busily preoccupied with their own desires and gratifications. He gains his spiritual authority by a lofty impartiality, becoming within *The Waste Land* the equivalent of the omniscient narrator of a realist novel. Eliot's own note is in fact misleading here. It is not 'although' he is 'a mere spectator and not indeed a "character"' that Tiresias is so important, but precisely *because* of this. Because he does not act, because he has no practical interests to defend, Tiresias achieves the impersonality that allows him to transcend the more sordid, self-interested perspectives of others. He represents what we might term a French or Mediterranean lucidity of intellect, in contrast to the more turbulently emotional Germanic or East European tones that elsewhere dominate the poem. Tiresias himself is a classical Greek figure, and it is a long passage from Ovid's Latin that Eliot offers us in the note as defining the context of his appearance in the poem. It is no accident that it is Mr Eugenides' 'invitation in demotic French' that immediately precedes Tiresias's arrival in the poem, just as, once he has departed from it, we gravitate back to Wagner's opera *Götterdämmerung* with the Thames-maidens' songs. Tiresias accordingly represents a last-ditch throw of classicist West European reason, with its ideals of balance, objectivity and lucidity, to encompass the post-war social crisis.

'What Tiresias *sees*, in fact, is the substance of the poem'. Being blind, however, he sees precisely *nothing* — and we should not, I think, be too quick to shift from a literal to a metaphorical meaning of 'seeing'. It is easy, perhaps too easy, to explain away Eliot's words by arguing that Tiresias is *morally* far-sighted, though physically disabled; I prefer here to linger on the harder implications of Eliot's phrase. Tiresias sees nothing, and in fact nothingness is his very mode of being; it is the price he has to pay for his effort to achieve a universal consciousness. He tries to be universal by containing opposites within himself, by always being *both* X *and* Y. In practice, however, this noble ambition turns out to mean *neither* X *nor* Y, and what looked like all-inclusiveness proves to be hollowness and negativity. 'Throbbing between two lives', Tiresias is no longer a man — he has 'wrinkled dugs' (l.228) — but is clearly not yet a woman; he is neither the one, nor the other.

Surveying the contemporary London scene, he is no longer a simple classical Greek, yet neither is he *fully* contemporary (otherwise tinned food wouldn't revolt him quite so much!). He is neither regal, though he associates with the legendary heroes of ancient Thebes, nor genuinely 'proletarian', though he has walked among the lowest of the dead — an experience which, as his contempt for modern working people shows, has done nothing whatsoever to teach him humility. This strangely negative mode of being, neither X nor Y, then infects every detail of the observed scene too. 'The evening hour' (l.220) is neither day nor night, the typist's divan is neither a real chair nor a real bed, and what takes place on it is not exactly rape, but neither is it 'real' — i.e. passionate, mutual — sex. To solve the postwar crisis, Tiresias must understand all partial viewpoints but give himself to none, and he turns himself into a Hollow Man in doing so. He must be indifferent to all the other characters, so that he can 'unite them all', but this then puts him in the same listless, passive position of the typist. The young man carbuncular deceives himself into taking her 'indifference' as a welcome, and the reader of the poem risks deceiving him or herself in the same way by taking Tiresias's indifference as a positive quality. Neither an aristocrat nor a member of the revolutionary 'hooded hordes', Tiresias seems initially as if he might be able to reconcile them. But in fact to be 'between two lives' (or in this case, social forces) in this way is simply to be a non-person, to have no substance or identity of one's own. Tiresias's inner emptiness can be felt in the rhythmic flatness and dryness of the lines he speaks. The project of social consensus which he embodies fails, and he fades from the poem, cast into historical irrelevance by the bitter social conflict of more powerful antagonists. If Tiresias *had* united all the other characters, the poem would have stopped there and then, triumphantly. The fact that it doesn't shows how little he achieves.

Once Tiresias fails, no *human* response to the crisis of the aristocracy is any longer possible. The hope for a solution has to be projected elsewhere, to a non-human source — rain or, more generally, Nature. Rain imagery in Eliot has often been misunderstood. Its conventional associations of freshness and soft, lush vegetation are replaced in his poetry by suggestions of martial hardness and social power. The best example of this is the opening of his 'Gerontion':

> Here I am, an old man in a dry month,
> Being read to by a boy, waiting for rain.

(ll.1–2)

These lines call up our conventional expectations — rain as gently nurturing, as soothing and dissolving a metallic sterility — but only in order to overthrow them, as when rain itself becomes almost a form of metal (the cutlass):

> I was neither at the hot gates
> Nor fought in the warm rain
> Nor knee deep in the salt marsh, heaving a cutlass,
> Bitten by flies, fought.

(ll.3–6)

Rain in Eliot is the energy of battle, that which allows you to challenge and defeat your political enemies. From the very beginning of *The Waste Land*, rain is associated with the aristocracy, as the shower surprises Marie in Munich. April rain, as we know, awakens 'memory and desire', and one powerful image in the aristocratic collective mind, both remembered *and* desired, is given in 'A Game of Chess':

> Above the antique mantel was displayed
> As though a window gave upon the sylvan scene
> The change of Philomel, by the barbarous king
> So rudely forced . . .

(ll.97–100)

'Barbarity' — an arrogant, reckless exercise of power — is precisely the characteristic of the traditional aristocracy, before it is 'undermined' by notions of human rights, democracy and so forth. The poem concedes that such masterful aggression is no longer a feasible response in the post-war world (this is, after all, an 'antique' mantel), and yet it simultaneously longs for such violence to be again possible.

The hectic, disordered visions of the poem's final section evoke social upheaval on a European scale. And the question posed by the Fisher King is, precisely, a *political* one: 'Shall I at least set my lands in order?' (l.425). Readings of *The Waste*

*Land* which interpret the poem as urging the need for inner, individual *moral* transformation seem to me not to do justice to the international range and ambition of this extraordinary text. The poem repeatedly stresses the need for the restoration of an entire social order:

> . . . upside down in air were towers
> Tolling reminiscent bells . . .

(ll.382–383)

As the adjective suggests, we are once more in the realm of 'memory and desire'. What is evoked here by the bells and towers is the image of a traditional aristocracy, secure in its own power and charisma, which was given in 'The Fire Sermon':

> Elizabeth and Leicester
> Beating oars
> The stern was formed
> A gilded shell
> . . .
> Southwest wind
> Carried down stream
> The peal of bells
> White towers

(ll.279–282; 286–289)

The current political menace is itself evoked in this vein of imagery in the poem's last lines. If the rain doesn't fall, giving the aristocracy the will and energy to reclaim its ancient authority — if necessary by military force — then the Fisher King faces the unenviable prospect of becoming '*Le Prince d'Aquitaine à la tour abolie*' (l.429), the disinherited man of Nerval's poem.

But the damp gust *does* bring rain, whether 'over Himavant' (l.397) or 'over the Starnbergersee' — just enough, at any rate, for the thunder to speak. What it declares must again, I think, be interpreted politically rather than morally. 'The awful daring' (l.403) which is contrasted to an 'age of prudence' (l.404) evokes the traditional aristocratic values of recklessness, largesse, *brio*, 'living dangerously', as against the petty, shopkeeperly mentality of the middle class. Social leadership is then restored:

> . . . your heart would have responded
> Gaily, when invited, beating obedient
> To controlling hands
>
> (ll.420–422)

There is to be no more post-war truculence; aristocratic charisma now compels immediate obedience. It is apt that this should be linked to the imagery of sea and sailors — 'The boat responded gaily' — which so permeates the poem. For in several instances, a crucial moment of the post-war revolutionary process was the mutiny of the fleet, when Stetson and all the others 'who were with me in the ships at Mylae' (l.70) decided, like Albert, that after four years in the forces they deserved 'a good time' — or at least a rather better time than their rulers were likely to give them. In the thunder's second speech these latent suggestions come to the fore, in the lines which are completely resistant to any moralising interpretation of the poem:

> Only at nightfall, aethereal rumours
> Revive for a moment a broken Coriolanus
>
> (ll.415–416)

The 'broken images' of the poem's first section were already the jumbled memories and experiences of an Austrian aristocrat. Now they are put back together in the powerful but disturbing figure of Coriolanus, the patrician hero of Shakespeare's play, a die-hard aristocrat deeply contemptuous of the Roman people or 'mob', believer in iron social and military discipline. Only a figure of this stature, the poem suggests, could effectively take on the Lenins and Trotskys at the head of those East European hooded hordes. The ambition to revive a broken Coriolanus or aristocracy seems to me to be at the very heart of Eliot's poem, just as it is of other modernist writers like Yeats and Lawrence. Readings of *The Waste Land* which begin by being too general, because they talk about 'modern man' rather than the post-war situation, end by being too narrow, because they see the poem as recommending an individual and moral, rather than social, solution to the crisis. A historical reading which respects the poem's immersion in its own present can, as I hope to have shown, avoid both these extremes.

# AFTERTHOUGHTS

Pinkney is deliberately controversial in the first paragraph of this essay. What effect does this have?

2

What evidence do you find in support of Pinkney's claim that Eliot was a 'diehard conservative' (page 23)? Is it necessary for a reader to share a poet's political beliefs?

3

Compare Pinkney's view of Tiresias (pages 25–27) with the views of Saunders (pages 37–38) and Wilson (pages 89–90).

4

Discuss the differences between Pinkney's interpretation of rain in *The Waste Land* (pages 27–29) and the interpretation offered by Mills (pages 68–69).

**John Saunders**

*John Saunders is Lecturer in English
Literature at the West Sussex Institute of
Higher Education, and an Awarder for
English Literature A-level with the
Oxford and Cambridge Schools
Examination Board.*

ESSAY

# The problem of time in *The Waste Land*

Integral to Eliot's vision of a disintegrating modern world is the
limited, fragmentary sense of time experienced by the men and
women who inhabit *The Waste Land*. As caged city dwellers
they live out of harmony with the seasons; as the inheritors of
a Europe devastated by war they live entirely in the present,
at best dimly aware of their cultural heritage and blind or
indifferent to the future; as heirs to the scientific revolutions of
the nineteenth century they are ignorant of any form of time
which transcends human measurement. This essay begins with
a consideration of natural, or seasonal time, moves on to
consider Eliot's treatment of linear time (present, past and
future) and ends with an exploration of religious or transcendental time. Though the poem itself makes no such tidy divisions, this plan will be following the overall structure of *The
Waste Land* as perceived by Ezra Pound when he described it
as 'the longest poem in the Englisch langwidge' running from
'"April . . ." to "shantih" without a break' (meaning here from
'spring' to 'eternity').

The Waste Land begins with four lines which but for one
word might be read as a traditional evocation of spring:

April is the cruellest month, breeding
Lilacs out of the dead land, mixing
Memory and desire, stirring
Dull roots with spring rain.

(ll.1–4)

Here the musical rhythm of the lines, the driving syntax (the first three lines ending in present participles) and the diction ('April', 'Lilacs', 'Memory and desire', 'spring rain') suggest an energetic and lyrical celebration of spring. Change 'cruellest' to 'kindest' and the lines would personify April as the bringer of new life and new beauty. However, the word 'cruellest' is the first of a series of indications of the disharmony of the seasons. It is not 'desire' which moves the poem forward with a new energy (as in Chaucer's Prologue to *The Canterbury Tales*) but 'memory' which dominates the lines which follow as the poem moves backward in time. Through the power of memory the seasons are set in reverse as we move back through winter ('warm' and 'forgetful') into a lyrical memory of a previous summer:

Summer surprised us, coming over the Starnbergersee
With a shower of rain; we stopped in the colonnade,
And went on in sunlight, into the Hofgarten

(ll.8–10)

Then, as this memory gives way to an even more indulgent nostalgia, the move through time continues back into a long-lost childhood winter:

And when we were children, staying at the arch-duke's,
My cousin's, he took me out on a sled,
And I was frightened. He said, Marie,
Marie, hold on tight. And down we went.
In the mountains, there you feel free.

(ll.13–17)

Marie's reminiscences of her aristocratic past may momentarily entrance the reader. The line which follows, however, reminds us that time has moved forward, not backward, as we find ourselves returned with a jolt to an unwelcoming present where the speaker's neurosis and rootlessness are shown in an attempt to evade natural time:

> I read, much of the night, and go south in the winter.

(l.18)

Though the opening lines of the poem may suggest that in spite of Marie's inclination to live in the past and to escape from winter, the cycle of the seasons will continue and April, however cruel, will return to replenish the earth, the second sub-section of the poem places Marie and her world in a spiritual 'dead land', the drought of a metaphorical summer which has known no spring:

> What are the roots that clutch, what branches grow
> Out of this stony rubbish? Son of man,
> You cannot say, or guess, for you know only
> A heap of broken images, where the sun beats,
> And the dead tree gives no shelter, the cricket no relief,
> And the dry stone no sound of water. . . .

(ll.19–24)

Here the poem suggests that modern — or Waste Land — man's dislocation from the rhythm of the seasonal year is but a symptom of a more significant spiritual dislocation of which he is unaware. In these lines the poem's voice becomes that of an Old Testament prophet, a voice which will return in the closing section, 'What the Thunder said', where once again the poem is set in a symbolic summer waiting for rain.

Lesser prophets preside over the middle sections of the poem: prophets more concerned with linear than with spiritual time. In fact, Eliot's concern with prophecy and the role of the poet is announced, somewhat enigmatically, in the epigraph which precedes the poem. Translated, this epigraph reads as follows:

> For I myself saw with my own eyes a certain Sybil of Cumae hanging in a cage, and when the boys said to her, 'Sybil, what do you desire?' she answered, 'I wish to die'.

In the story of the Sybil of Cumae, Eliot found an image which both encapsulated the dislocation of present, past and future time which he saw as symptomatic of the cultural plight of modern man and which parallelled his own plight as a modern poet. In Greek mythology Sibyls were women endowed with prophetic power, the power to see into the future. The Cumaean Sybil had been famed both for her prophecy and for her beauty. So beautiful had she been that she was loved by Apollo, who promised to grant her eternal youth if she succumbed to his advances. She refused, but when Apollo promised to grant her anything she wished without conditions, she pointed to a mound of earth and asked to be given a year of life for each grain of sand it contained. Ironically she did not look to the future and failed to ask for youth to accompany her age. As she grew older and older both her memory and her prophetic power faded. Caged in the present she was only dimly aware of her mythical, magical past and quite indifferent to the future. As such, living in a seemingly eternal present, her fate anticipated the fates of the inhabitants of *The Waste Land*.

Though *The Waste Land* ranges freely in time and place, images of London in the aftermath of the First World War — the London in which Eliot lived for much of the time that he was writing the poem — provide a re-occurring present tense for the poem. The inhabitants of this London know only a 'heap of broken images' (l.22). Their sense of the past is fragmentary, disconnected and insignificant. If they have a sense of the future it is through the mumbo jumbo of figures like Madame Sosostris, who play at prophecy. London, as the centre of *The Waste Land*, is unambiguously introduced in the lines which begin the final sub-section of 'The Burial of the Dead':

> Unreal City,
> Under the brown fog of a winter dawn,
> A crowd flowed over London Bridge, so many,
> I had not thought death had undone so many.
>
> (ll.60–63)

In cinematic terms this may be regarded as a 'long shot'. In the two sections which follow, Eliot provides a series of 'close-ups' anatomising the spiritual condition of London and his Londoners.

Following the baroque setting which introduces 'A Game of Chess' the reader, not unlike a voyeur, experiences the neurotic tensions of the 'she' of the opening lines as she talks to her companion:

> My nerves are bad to-night. Yes, bad. Stay with me.
> Speak to me. Why do you never speak. Speak.
>
> (ll.111–112)

In the duologue which ensues, the neurosis is shown to be closely related to time. The couple seem to be in a void, in a present cut off from past and future:

>                                    Do
> You know nothing? Do you see nothing? Do you remember
> Nothing?
>
> (ll.121–123)

Within this void, life has no purpose:

> What shall I do now? What shall I do?
>     . . .
>                         . . . What shall we do tomorrow?
> What shall we ever do?
>
> (ll.131–134)

The companion's answer suggests the futility of a bandaged existence made up of comfortable, time-passing rituals which insulate their participants from life itself but fail to protect them from the menace of the future:

> The hot water at ten.
> And if it rains, a closed car at four.
> And we shall play a game of chess,
> Pressing lidless eyes and waiting for a knock upon the door.
>
> (ll.134–137)

The paucity of the present and the menace of the future continue through the sub-section which follows. While the speaker tells with relish the story of the sordid love life of Lil and Albert (Lil's toothlessness, her five unwanted children, her abortion and her premature old age; Albert's need for 'a good time' following his four years in the army, his reluctance to look at Lil and his refusal to leave her alone), the barman's repeated calls, printed in block capitals, take on a prophetic urgency, hinting at an impending doom:

HURRY UP PLEASE ITS TIME

. . .

HURRY UP PLEASE ITS TIME

. . .

HURRY UP PLEASE ITS TIME
HURRY UP PLEASE ITS TIME

(ll.152,165,169,170)

Though there are hints here and in the final section of *The Waste Land* of an imminent apocalypse — of 'hooded hordes' swarming across Europe, of 'Falling towers' in some of the world's most civilised cities, of 'London Bridge' falling down — for much of the poem it is the pressure of the past, not the future, which is brought to bear on the present. In the central section of the poem, 'The Fire Sermon', the linking of present and past is achieved through the figure of Tiresias. In classical mythology Tiresias was distinctive for having experienced life (and love) both as a man and a woman. (A passage from Ovid in Eliot's 'Notes on the Waste Land' explains how the trans-formation came about.) When Jove and Juno (king and queen of the gods on Mount Olympus) debated the question as to whether man or woman derived most pleasure from sex, they appealed to Tiresias as a witness. His answer, 'woman', so infuriated Juno that she struck him blind. In compensation Jove (who was delighted by the verdict) gave him the power of prophecy. In *The Waste Land* it is Tiresias's knowledge of the past, not the future, which is utilised. 'What Tiresias *sees*,' Eliot tells us in his Notes is 'the substance of the poem'. What he sees is yet another sterile human relationship: the seduction of 'the typist' by a 'small house agent's clerk' (ll.220–256). The scene is set firmly in time and place on a winter evening in a small London bed-sitting room. It is described in some detail, each detail depriving the encounter of any glamour or passion. The typist returns from her work, clears away her breakfast, lights the stove and 'lays out food in tins'. Outside the window hang her 'drying combinations'. On her divan ('at night her bed') are 'stockings, slippers, camisoles, and stays'. Her guest arrives. He is 'the young man carbuncular'. After the meal she, though 'bored and tired', does not resist his advances. There is no desire or love in their coupling: she is passive and indifferent; he is driven not by lust but by the vanity of his male ego. Following a weary account of their loveless love-making. Tiresias gives the reader a brief reminder of his own mythical past:

> I who have sat by Thebes below the wall
> And walked among the lowest of the dead.

(ll.245–246)

Here the reference to Thebes should remind us of Tiresias's role in the story of Oedipus where, called upon to reveal the reason why Thebes had become infertile and racked with disease, Tiresias rightly saw this earlier 'waste land' as resulting from Oedipus's having unknowingly killed his father (Laius) and married his mother (Jocasta). In this allusive reference to 'Thebes', Tiresias/Eliot juxtaposes the seemingly insignificant modern episode of the typist's seduction with one of the Greek myths which has continued to haunt the imagination of Western Europe. What is the effect of this juxtaposition? Does it show that there have been other waste lands? or contrast the grandeur of the myth with the banality of the present? To some extent here, as in the rest of the poem, readers are forced to make their own associations, which will depend partly on their own knowledge of the mythic moments to which the poem alludes.

Though in the central section of 'The Fire Sermon' it is ostensibly Tiresias who employs 'the mythical method' juxtaposing the present with a mythical past, for the remainder of the poem it is Eliot himself who performs this function. The sterility of the modern waste land is emphasised through a range of parallels and contrasts as Eliot draws on his magpie-like knowledge of European culture and world religions. Several of the quotations from European writers which contribute to the collage-like form of the poem are clearly foregrounded since they are not in English: fragments from the libretto to *Tristan and Isolde*, lines from Baudelaire, Verlaine, Dante and de Nerval. Others are embedded in the text as translations or near translations and, together with the quotations or near quotations from English poetry, they establish a richly subtle and allusive network of references which Eliot uses throughout the poem to highlight the sterility of London, of London life and of London relationships. So, in the opening passage where the London scene is set, the words 'Unreal City' are taken from Baudelaire while the line 'I had not thought death had undone so many' is a direct echo of the moment in Dante's *Inferno* where Dante first sees the souls of the dead. Here Baudelaire's and Dante's visions parallel and reinforce Eliot's vision and, perhaps more significantly, elevate his status as a seer. More generally the parallels work through contrast and often to appreciate their full significance the reader needs to bring to Eliot's text a detailed knowledge of the earlier texts to which he is alluding. The opening lines of 'A Game of Chess', for example, are a grotesque parody of Shakespeare's magnificent account (based on Plutarch) of the first meeting between Antony and Cleopatra. Any reader should sense that there is something unwholesome and claustrophobic in Eliot's description of the ornate interior where 'she' prepares for the arrival of her companion:

> The Chair she sat in, like a burnished throne,
> Glowed on the marble, where the glass
> Held up by standards wrought with fruited vines
> From which a golden Cupidon peeped out
> (Another hid his eyes behind his wing)
> Doubled the flames of sevenbranched candelabra
> Reflecting light upon the table as
> The glitter of her jewels rose to meet it,
> From satin cases poured in rich profusion.
> In vials of ivory and coloured glass
> Unstoppered, lurked her strange synthetic perfumes,
> Unguent, powdered, or liquid — troubled, confused
> And drowned the sense in odours . . .
>
> (ll.77–89)

To appreciate the full force of the parody (and to appreciate many of its details) it is necessary to measure Eliot's cloying image of modern degradation against the freshness and vitality of the earlier meeting to which it repeatedly refers. In Shakespeare's play this is a moment where present, past and future meet to transcend time: it occurs midway through *Antony and Cleopatra* as, through the voice of Enobarbus, Shakespeare creates in his audience's minds a vivid image of the meeting on the river Cydnus, which will be evoked again when, at her death, Cleopatra declares:

                    I am again for Cydnus
To meet Mark Antony.

                                            (V.2.228–229)

This is the moment to which Cleopatra is referring, an image
wrought out of gold and silver and the 'higher' medieval
elements — fire, air and water:

> The barge she sat in, like a burnish'd throne,
> Burnt on the water. The poop was beaten gold,
> Purple the sails, and so perfumed that
> The winds were love-sick with them; the oars were silver,
> Which to the tune of flutes kept stroke, and made
> The water which they beat to follow faster,
> As amorous of their strokes. For her own person,
> It beggar'd all description: she did lie
> In her pavilion — cloth of gold, of tissue —
> O'er-picturing that Venus where we see
> The fancy outwork nature. On each side her
> Stood pretty dimpled boys, like smiling Cupids,
> With divers-colour'd fans, whose winds did seem
> To glow the delicate cheeks which they did cool,
> And what they undid did.

                                            (II.2.190–204)

A more general and much more complex contrast between
present and past centres on the symbol of the river Thames as
it flows through 'The Fire Sermon'. The section begins with a
depressing picture of the modern river in winter:

> The river's tent is broken; the last fingers of leaf
> Clutch and sink into the wet bank. The wind
> Crosses the brown land, unheard. The nymphs are departed.
> Sweet Thames, run softly, till I end my song.
> The river bears no empty bottles, sandwich papers,
> Silk handkerchiefs, cardboard boxes, cigarette ends
> Or other testimony of summer nights. The nymphs are departed.
> And their friends, the loitering heirs of city directors;
> Departed, have left no addresses.

                                            (ll.173–181)

To the uninformed reader the references to 'The nymphs' and

the incongruous lyricism of the line 'Sweet Thames, run softly, till I end my song' will work only at the level of bitter sarcasm. For a full appreciation of their significance it is necessary to recognise their source in Spenser's 'Prothalamion', where 'Sweet Thames, run softly, till I end my song' is a choral refrain, ending each of the nine stanzas. 'Prothalamion' was written in 1596 to celebrate the marriages of the daughters of the Earl of Worcester. A magical, flower-adorned, 'silver streaming Thames' flows through Spenser's poem, the river becoming a symbol of wholesome fertility as the river nymphs, 'lovely daughters of the flood', prepare posies for their own weddings and then bedeck a pair of snow-white swans who — symbolic of the perfection of marriage — glide down the river to the palace where the Earl waits with his daughters. In Eliot's poem the Thames is filthy and the 'nymphs' — like the Thames-daughters in the lines which are to follow — have used it for their sordid, clandestine sexual encounters. In contrast to Spenser's swans, the only life which stirs on the 'winter evening behind the gas house' which Eliot chooses for his setting is the rat which:

> . . . crept softly through the vegetation
> Dragging its slimy belly on the bank.

(ll.187–188)

The Thames returns to the poem in the closing sub-section of 'The Fire Sermon', which Eliot in his Notes refers to as 'The Song of the (three) Thames-daughters'. Here the contrast between present and past is, at least rhythmically, less marked as the modern setting with its 'Oil and tar' and its drifting barges gives way to a Renaissance love affair which did not end in marriage:

> Elizabeth and Leicester
> Beating oars
> The stern was formed
> A gilded shell
> Red and gold
> The brisk swell
> Rippled both shores
> Southwest wind
> Carried down stream

The peal of bells
White towers
Weialala leia
Wallala leialala

(ll.279–292)

The chorus here, the:

Weialala leia
Wallala leialala

is taken from the lament of the Rhine-maidens in *Die Götterdämmerung* and serves to parallel the sterility of the modern Thames with the Rhine which, in Wagner's operatic treatment of the German legend, had lost its beauty through the theft of the river's gold ('The Ring', which gives its name to the operatic cycle of which *Die Götterdämmerung* is the final part). In the opera the curse on the river is about to end with the ring's return to the maidens, and the opera, following the death of Siegfried, is about to end in the redemptive triumph of love. In Eliot's poem there is at this point little hint of redemption, the movement ending as the three 'Thames-daughters' tell in turn the stories of their own violations: the first losing her virginity 'Supine on the floor of a narrow canoe' at 'Richmond', the second being undone at 'Moorgate', the third 'On Margate Sands' (Richmond, Moorgate and Margate all being on the Thames estuary). With the story of the third Thames-daughter the poem reaches its nihilistic nadir, past and future offering 'Nothing' and existence reduced to a single memory of ugliness:

On Margate Sands.
I can connect
Nothing with nothing.
The broken fingernails of dirty hands.
My people humble people who expect
Nothing.

(ll.300–305)

The reader who has followed Eliot's allusions will have a range of connections with which to evaluate the vacuity of such an existence. However, the literary and cultural references which measure the present against the past have at this point little to offer by way of redemption. From this point in the poem a different set of associations from the past work towards an ending which, if not redemptive, is not entirely bleak. These are the many references to forgotten or outmoded religious cults. Madame Sosostris is the focal point for these images in the first half of the poem. In looking to the future she plays with her Tarot pack, referring mysteriously to a number of cards which, for Eliot, had a mythical significance as obscure traces of pre-Christian cults. The cards which refer directly to these cults are 'the drowned Phoenician Sailor' and 'The Hanged Man'. Eliot became aware of the potential significance of these cards through his reading of Frazer's *The Golden Bough* (in particular the volumes dealing with ancient fertility cults centred on the figures of Adonis, Attis and Osiris) and through his reading of Jessie Weston's *From Ritual to Romance*, which he acknowledges in his Notes as the source of the poem's title and 'a good deal of the incidental symbolism'. Jessie Weston had argued that behind the many European stories of the legend of the Holy Grail (of which the tales of King Arthur and his Knights are an English manifestation) lay pre-Christian vegetation ceremonies in which the waste land of winter was, each year, ended through ritual sacrifice. Both 'the drowned Phoenician Sailor' and 'The Hanged Man' can be seen as precursors of Christ, whose crucifixion parallelled these more primitive sacrifices. *The Waste Land*'s preoccupation with sacrifice as a theme is obscurely alluded to in the lyrical moment in the Hyacinth garden, the hyacinth flower being a symbol of the resurrected god, whose name it bears. Sacrifice is hinted at in the title of the opening section, 'The Burial of the Dead', the section ending with a grotesque parody of sacrificial burial, present and past meeting incongruously as the poem's protagonist — here a survivor from the battle of Mylae, which took place in 260 BC — greets his friend Stetson outside a London church, Saint Mary Woolnoth, asking:

> That corpse you planted last year in your garden,
> Has it begun to sprout? Will it bloom this year?

> (ll.71–72)

Though there are other references to the idea of death and rebirth in the first three sections of the poem (the several allusions to *The Tempest* may be seen to fit into this pattern), it is in the last two sections that the theme of ritual sacrifice and renewal becomes central to the poem. Section IV, as its title, 'Death by Water', indicates, is given over to symbolic drowning. Phlebas is partly a modern merchant (like Mr Eugenides, concerned with 'profit and loss') and partly (as 'the drowned Phoenician Sailor') a manifestation of the god figure who in primitive cults died to redeem the winter waste land. Significantly, as the sea current picks his bones, Phlebas moves backwards in time, passing the 'stages of his youth'. Here the present and past come together, not grotesquely but meditatively, preparing for the final section of the poem, 'What the Thunder said', where we are once again in a spiritual waste land, waiting for rain. Image after image in this final section communicates an atmosphere of intolerable heat, where 'red sullen faces sneer and snarl', where a cave is a 'Dead mountain mouth of carious teeth that cannot spit', where the 'limp leaves' wait. Time and place keep shifting, the final moments of waiting being set in the valley of the Ganges — the home of the earliest vegetation cults. However, the central figure who presides over 'What the Thunder said' is not an earth mother or a pagan fertility god but Christ himself. The opening lines evoke the moment in time immediately after the crucifixion:

> After the torchlight red on sweaty faces
> After the frosty silence in the gardens
> After the agony in stony places
> The shouting and the crying
> Prison and palace and reverberation
> Of thunder and spring over distant mountains
> He who was living is now dead
> We who were living are now dying
> With a little patience

(ll.322–330)

The Christian imagery here is vivid and unambiguous. Christ was arrested in the garden of Gethsemane, the arresting party including (according to St John) men who came 'with lanterns and torches and weapons'. Following his arrest Christ was taken to prison, then to the palace of the High Priest before being tried by Pilate. At his death (according to St Matthew) the earth reverberated. Christian references continue as the poem alludes to the journey to Emmaus where, following the resurrection, two of the disciples encountered the resurrected Christ on the road but did not recognise him: ('Who is the third who walks always beside you'). There may be further Christian connotations in the cock's 'Co co rico co co rico' which in the poem precedes the 'flash of lightning' and the 'damp gust/Bringing rain'. Clearly in this symbolic drought-stricken landscape the 'rain' will bring with it not renewed fertility but its religious analogue, spiritual salvation.

However, the message of 'the thunder' introduces into the poem not Christian but Hindu teaching, shifting the focus from the vast panorama of the crouching jungle to the individual life. Though the *Datta ... Dayadhvam ... Damyata* ('Give', 'Sympathise', 'Control') as commands point to the future, they trigger in the mind of the protagonist personal memory ('What have we given') and cultural memory ('a broken Coriolanus') and they introduce into the poem for the first time the subjunctive mood, a poignant sense of what might have been:

> your heart would have responded
> Gaily, when invited, beating obedient
> To controlling hands

> (ll.420–422)

The shift from an objective denunciation of the sterility of the Waste Land to more subjective self-examination continues in the last eleven lines of the poem, where the previously perceived disintegration of the modern world becomes linked with the precarious instability of the protagonist's own mind as a succession of disordered, personally significant 'fragments' suggest incoherence and imminent mental breakdown. However, the last two lines give a hint of private redemption as the repeated 'Datta, Dayadhvam, Damyata' is followed by:

> Shantih shantih shantih

the words bringing with them the 'sound of water' for which we have been waiting and whose meaning, 'The Peace which passeth understanding', suggests that finally redemption will lie beyond time.

# AFTERTHOUGHTS

## 1

Saunders's essay distinguishes between 'linear' and 'transcendental' time. Consider how this distinction is reflected in the structure of his essay.

## 2

How helpful do you find it to consider *The Waste Land* in 'cinematic terms' (page 35)?

## 3

Compare Saunders's view of Tiresias (pages 37–38) with the views of Pinkney (pages 25–27) and Wilson (pages 89–90).

## 4

What 'further Christian connotations' (page 45) might there be in the crowing of the cock?

## Claire Saunders

*Claire Saunders teaches English at Lavant House, and has many years' experience as an A-level examiner. She has recently completed with John Saunders an edition of* The Duchess of Malfi *for the Longman Study Texts series.*

ESSAY

# Women and *The Waste Land*

Yes, AND. 'Women IN *The Waste Land*' is, admittedly, what I started with. Those varied glimpses of women, ranging from Mrs Porter and her daughter washing their feet in soda water to the etherial cry of the violated Philomel, demanded further exploration. But although there is a pleasure in sifting through *The Waste Land* like an archaeologist, sorting the images — broken or not — and labelling them, 'Women' can't really be sustained as a separate category. They aren't, after all, limited to 'she'. What of 'you' and 'we' and, especially, 'I'? The constantly shifting pronouns in *The Waste Land* challenge *me*. So I want to discuss not only women within T S Eliot's poem but also women in relation to the poem and the poet's viewpoint. But I shall start with, and concentrate on, the 'third person' women — those presented as dramatis personae.

    *The Waste Land* is, at the most immediately striking level, a sort of collage of human figures. In separating out the women I am applying the most original and fundamental of divisions — 'Male and female created he them', as Genesis has it. Subsequent divisions may distinguish human beings according to social, aesthetic, moral and other criteria but gender remains, apparently, the most obvious and crucial of identification tags. So it is at first easy to list the women in *The Waste Land*. In order of appearance they could be picked out as Marie, the

Hyacinth Girl, Madame Sosostris, the Woman-with-hairbrush, Philomel, Lil and her 'friend', Mrs Porter, the Typist, Elizabeth and the Thames-daughters. They certainly seem varied. Do they just constitute a cross-section of humanity? Carefully assembled fictional cross-sections — Chaucer's Canterbury pilgrims, for instance, or the sort of group gathered in an airport lounge for a 'disaster movie' — do not give women such prominence, for a start. Compared with the equivalent list of male figures in *The Waste Land* (the Arch-duke, Stetson, Albert, Sweeney, Mr Eugenides, the 'young man carbuncular', Leicester and Phlebas), Eliot's female figures are not only more numerous but also more vividly realised. Why? How do they affect the reader and what do they contribute to the poem?

The first woman defined in *The Waste Land* is Marie (ll.8–18). It is not really clear when she is established as a dramatic character because she seems to emerge from the opening 'we' of the poem. Her name is revealed as she recalls a moment of frightened ecstacy:

> And when we were children, staying at the arch-duke's,
> My cousin's, he took me out on a sled,
> And I was frightened. He said, Marie,
> Marie, hold on tight. And down we went.

> (ll.13–16)

This past experience is linked ('mixing/ Memory with desire') with a present yearning: 'In the mountains, there you feel free.' The adult Marie is socially well established, outwardly secure, but she is inwardly restless, unsatisfied: 'I read much of the night, and go south in the winter.' Despite her self-assertiveness ('Bin gar keine Russin, stamm' aus Litauen, echt deutsch,') Eliot's portrait is of someone deeply insecure. Marie seems to me to represent not only the European aristocracy shaken by the social and political upheaval of the First World War but everyone, man or woman, whose apparently flourishing existence is, in fact, rootless.

The evocation of Marie leads straight into the poet's search for something more sustaining:

> What are the roots that clutch, what branches grow
> Out of this stony rubbish? . . .

> (ll.19–20)

Madame Sosostris, 'known to be the wisest woman in Europe', might be expected to give an answer. But Eliot's portrait (ll.43–59) is of someone ludicrous, perhaps a little sinister, but certainly not authoritative. The pretentious introduction, 'Madame Sosostris, famous clairvoyante', is swiftly undercut by 'Had a bad cold'; the session ends in precious banality:

> . . . If you see dear Mrs Equitone,
> Tell her I bring the horoscope myself:
> One must be so careful these days.
>
> (ll.57–59)

And Madame Sosostris disappears, a cameo expressive of the hollowness of such dabblings in the occult. Her soothsayer phrases ('I do not find/ The Hanged Man. Fear death by water') reverberate through the poem, but she is a device rather than a character.

With neither of these two figures in 'The Burial of the Dead' does the fact that they are women seem crucial. It is quite otherwise in the second and third parts of *The Waste Land*. 'A Game of Chess', in particular, is absolutely dominated by two dramatic portraits. Though contrasted in almost every possible way, the two main figures have a common bond: their misery seems to be firmly associated with their sexual and social identity as women. The first woman (ll.77–138) — nameless — is presented at her dressing-table. Her hair, as she brushes it:

> Spread out in fiery points
> Glowed into words, then would be savagely still.
>
> (ll.109–110)

The words which spurt out from her are exclamations, questions. They express nervous dissatisfaction and a sense of panic: 'Stay with me . . . Why do you never speak? . . . What are you thinking of? . . . What is that noise? . . . What shall I do?' She is involved in a one-sided dialogue. Whose is the other voice? The setting suggests a husband or lover but his words are not punctuated as direct speech — he is not really an equal partner in the drama, more a tormenting presence. The dressing-room is revealed as richly claustrophobic: shiny surfaces and glittering jewels infinitely reflect the flickering light and the atmosphere is of 'strange, synthetic perfumes'. Eliot's original title for this section was 'In the Cage': this woman is trapped. She flares up, imagining escape:

> I shall rush out as I am, and walk the street
> With my hair down, so.

> (ll.132–133)

But immediately she subsides again into hopelessness — 'What shall we ever do?' She is answered by the firmly restrictive vision of her future:

> The hot water at ten,
> And if it rains, a closed car at four,
> And we shall play a game of chess,
> Pressing lidless eyes and waiting for a knock upon the door.

> (ll.135–138)

The game of chess recalls most notably a scene from a play (Middleton's *Women Beware Women*) in which a chess-game systematically patterns out the seduction of a young woman. Eliot's Woman-with-hairbrush is identified, through allusion and quotation, with a whole company of heroines who were also victims. The references to Cleopatra, Dido, Eve and Ophelia are noted by B C Southam (*A Student's Guide to the Selected Poems of T. S. Eliot* (London, 1968)) but there is also the Duchess of Malfi (a poem entitled 'The Death of the Duchess', linking this dressing-table scene with Webster's play, is attached to the manuscript of *The Waste Land*). The most pitiful evocation is of Philomel, the woman brutally raped whose sad story is literally framed within the dressing-room scene of her unhappy successor. Although in Ovid the 'change of Philomel' is the beautiful metamorphosis of violated victim into nightingale, in Eliot's poem the resolution seems unsuccessful:

> . . . yet there the nightingale
> Filled all the desert with inviolable voice
> And still she cried, and still the world pursues,
> 'Jug Jug' to dirty ears.

> (ll.100–103)

'Jug Jug', simultaneously an innocent evocation of bird-song and a crude reference to sexual intercourse, is repeated as the figure of Philomel is recalled in the third section of *The*

*Waste Land.* But before that there is Lil, the second woman found trapped in 'A Game of Chess' (ll.139–172). Lil's position is obviously grim and hopeless. Utterly worn down by poverty, child-bearing and abortion, she is nevertheless expected to make herself 'a bit smart' and give Albert 'a good time', her nagging 'friend' all the time poised to gobble up her husband along with the hot gammon. The friend seems brashly confident but, as the pub 'goonight's' modulate into Ophelia's final farewell ('Goodnight, sweet ladies'), we realise that she and Lil are both objects of pity: with Time remorselessly against them they cannot look for happiness in the corrupting world of sensuality.

Not all the women are sufferers. Mrs Porter and her daughter, feet plunged in washing soda, are figures from a brothel in a song sung by soldiers. Their cheerful, solid coarseness is ironically counterpointed by the 'voix d'enfants, chantant dans la coupole'; these children sing at a ritual foot-washing ceremony in the story of a virgin knight! 'The Fire Sermon', the third part of *The Waste Land*, is centred on sensuality as denounced by Buddha and St Augustine, Eastern and Western representatives of the ascetic vocation. Eliot's manuscript of the poem shows that he had intended to start this section with a portrait of a woman, Fresca, composed in the style of Pope's 'Rape of the Lock'. Although the lines were vetoed by Eliot's friend and critic, Ezra Pound, Eliot himself thought they were an excellent set of couplets. Pound was surely right. They remind me more of Swift than of Pope, showing an almost obsessive physical revulsion as Eliot follows Fresca's morning 'toilet':

> . . . to the steaming bath she moves,
> Her tresses fanned by little flutt'ring Loves;
> Odours, confected by the cunning French,
> Disguise the good old hearty female stench.

Something of this harsh yet prurient disgust remains in the central satirical passage of *The Waste Land*, the seduction of the Typist (ll.215–256). She is sketched in terms of her sordid physical background:

> The typist home at teatime, clears her breakfast, lights
> Her stove, and lays out food in tins.

Out of the window perilously spread
Her drying combinations touched by the sun's last rays,
On the divan are piled (at night her bed)
Stockings, slippers, camisoles, and stays.

(ll.222–227)

The expected guest — bold, patronising, yet also pathetic, initiates the 'assault'. The whole episode is tawdry and depressing and the phrases which express the woman's response thump wearily at the ends of lines: 'tired . . . undesired . . . no defence . . . indifference'. The fine emotions of Goldsmith's Olivia, the original of 'When lovely woman stoops to folly' (*The Vicar of Wakefield*), are shrivelled to an empty gesture:

She smoothes her hair with automatic hand,
And puts a record on the gramophone.

(ll.255–256)

The music which 'crept by me upon the waters' returns the reader to the river, which is the setting for most of 'The Fire Sermon'. The opening lines (ll.173–181) had painted a sad autumnal River Thames from which 'the nymphs are departed'; the next woman seems to transform the scene. Like a carnival float — or one of her own processional pageants — the Queen Elizabeth tableau (ll.279–289) passes lightly by. The short, loosely constucted lines are like jottings for a film-sketch. Eliot's note draws our attention to a particular incident of regal flirtation, and one could see this as another episode of sterile sexuality, but I find that the tableau has a decorative rather than a dramatic impact. The Elizabeth and Leicester section is the second of a pair of poems which share the same form and the same lamenting refrain. The first poem (ll.266–76) paints a beautifully sombre scene:

The river sweats
Oil and tar
The barges drift
With the turning tide

Elizabeth's contrasting scene is gaily extravagant; the 'gilded shell/ Red and gold' is briskly propelled in a picture-book setting. Later the 'peal of bells/ White towers' will be scarily transformed — 'upside down in air were towers/ Tolling reminiscent bells' (ll.382–383) — but here the effect is of a romantic past focused on an appropriately picturesque woman — Gloriana, the Virgin Queen; she has little to do with the present reality of the waste land.

In fact Elizabeth is not an independent figure in *The Waste Land* but is, according to Eliot's note, part of the 'Song of the (three) Thames-daughters' — consisting of the two Thames scenes and three specific Thames incidents, of girls being casually violated. The direction that the three incidents should be individually narrated indicates that the Thames-daughters are to be seen as dramatic figures. Within the poem they seem to be three manifestations of a single phenomenon, differentiated mainly by their association with different reaches of the river. The first is undone by Richmond and Kew, the sexual act sounding banal, matter-of-fact:

> . . . I raised my knees
> Supine on the floor of a narrow canoe.

(ll.294–295)

For the second (ll.296–305) the 'event' happens at Moorgate. The man is emptily penitent; the girl is dully unimpressed — 'What should I resent?' The third, on Margate Sands, is more articulate. Despite her negative 'I can connect/ Nothing with nothing', her sharp focus on the lover — 'The broken fingernails of dirty hands' — suggests all too well the dreary prospect for her kind: 'My people humble people who expect/ Nothing.' (ll.304–305). All three are unresisting, unprotesting. Yet to the reader of *The Waste Land* their song *is* a protest because the individual stories are ironically set within a general imaginative context. In referring to the women as 'Thames-daughters' Eliot evokes Spenser's 'Daughters-of-the-Flood', the happy Thames nymphs who honour the bridal day in the 'Prothalamion' (a poem already summoned in the borrowed line 'Sweet Thames run softly till I end my song'). Eliot's modern nymphs have no happy wedding to celebrate. Their desolation is defined through their song's refrain:

> Weialala leia
> Wallala leialala

This is the cry of those other water-nymphs, the Rhine-maidens from Wagner's opera-cycle *The Ring*, who cry for the loss of the gold which has assured and symbolised their beauty. The nymphs of *The Waste Land* are denied a final lyrical expression of grief at their own violation — just the sad 'la la', an insignificant echo of the Rhine-maidens' lament.

So the procession of women in *The Waste Land* ends. The voice of St Augustine which concludes the third part implies that women are to be dismissed as corrupt, a sensual distraction — 'To Carthage then I came, where a cauldron of unholy loves sang all about mine ears' (ll.307–308 and Eliot's note). Apart from the 'Murmur of maternal lamentation' (l.367) and the nightmarish 'A woman drew her long black hair out tight' (l.377) — perhaps a guilty memory to torment the protagonist of 'What the Thunder said' — there seems to be no place for women in the final parts of the journey through the waste land. All the women of any substance in the first three parts, the women who engage the reader, have been objects to reject or pity. But there is one notable exception — the one figure not yet discussed.

The Hyacinth Girl (ll.35–42) differs from the others in that she is presented in the second person — she is 'you' not 'she'. The poet describes her while addressing her:

> . . . when we came back, late, from the Hyacinth garden,
> Your arms full, and your hair wet . . .

Striking similarities with Eliot's early and most romantically lyrical of poems, 'La Figlia che Piange', reinforce the sense that this moment, this encounter, is of crucial significance. She introduces herself:

> You gave me hyacinths first a year ago;
> They called me the hyacinth girl.

At a probably trivial level of realism I can't help finding this voice coy. However hyacinth, the mythical flower of resurrection, recalling the myth of Adonis, suggests that this episode is far more symbolic than real. The poet proceeds to recount an almost mystical experience:

> . . . I could not
> Speak, and my eyes failed, I was neither
> Living nor dead, and I knew nothing,
> Looking into the heart of light, the silence.

The moment of enlightenment is not sustained, giving way to empty desolation — '*Oed' und leer das Meer'*. Yet the language suggests that the Hyacinth Girl could almost be a Beatrice to Eliot's Dante — the blessed woman who can guide the poet to his vision of heaven. One can link the Hyacinth Girl, offering a glimpse of possible communication, to an almost hopeful passage at the end of the poem:

> The sea was calm, your heart would have responded
> Gaily, when invited, beating obedient
> To controlling hands

> (ll.420–422)

Assuming that this cooperative figure is also female, it is tempting to see the 'you' woman as Eliot's positive, a woman hinting at redemption for the male poet struggling through the waste land of 'unholy loves'. Are all the other women of *The Waste Land* — trivial, sordid or pathetic — to be set against this one?

The polarisation of female characters — either pure or impure — has long been a male chiché observable in writers who have not come to terms with the reality of women. On one level *The Waste Land* can be seen as the 'rhythmical grumbling' (Eliot's own words) of a man suffering some sort of emotional and spiritual breakdown and those who defy Eliot's plea against biographical investigation can find plenty of evidence for a sexual dimension to the poet's troubled state. (See P Ackroyd's *T. S. Eliot* (London, 1984) and M Hastings's play *Tom and Viv*). But there is certainly no question of simplistic male chauvinism. Eliot shows great sensitivity and subtlety — both in *The Waste Land* and in other poems – in his portraits of women. What is striking in *The Waste Land* is that it is the women who do all the immediate, actual suffering. This is odd because it runs counter to the mythical basis of the poem (an amalgam of ancient fertility rites and legends found largely in *The Golden Bough* and *From Ritual to Romance*). Redemption — the bringing of water to the barren (female) land — traditionally features the sacrifice of a male god or hero. In *The Waste Land*, however, the sacrificial victims are most definitely female and unheroic. Eliot may have sensed this when deciding to change the original epigraph to the poem. Although in the final version 'In the Cage' is no longer the title to the second section, the image of a woman trapped in a state of suffering is eloquently captured in the new Latin epigraph — a picture of the Sibyl of Cumae:

> For once I saw with my very own eyes the Sibyl at Cumae hanging in a cage, and when the boys said to her, 'Sibyl, what do you want?' she answered 'I want to die.'

Sibylla was actually the pen-name used by T S Eliot's first wife, Vivien. Although she has been identified by a friend of Eliot's as his 'muse' or source of poetic inspiration, her own unhappiness was also a major cause of his sense of personal failure. It is the Sibyl of Cumae, compelled to suffer to eternity, who introduces the poem and sets its tone. She speaks, perhaps, for all the sad, wasted women in Eliot's waste land.

The Sibyl's female voice is not, however, the main voice of the poem. In a letter Eliot signed himself, jokingly, 'Tiresias' and it is this legendary prophet who is at the centre of the poem:

> I Tiresias, though blind, throbbing between two lives,
> Old man with wrinkled female breasts, can see

> (ll.218–219)

The attributes of blindness, longevity and prophetic power all, according to Ovid's version of the legend, result from the fact that Tiresias had spent seven years of his life as a woman. He is, therefore, a figure who transcends gender. Eliot spells it out for the reader in his apparently most eager-to-help note:

> Tiresias, although a mere spectator and not indeed a 'character', is yet the most important personage in the poem, uniting all the rest ... the two sexes meet in Tiresias. What Tiresias *sees*, in fact, is the substance of the poem.

Does this then mean that the main voice of the poem, the 'I', is both male and female? Eliot's use of the first person pronoun is constructively confused. The first pronoun of the poem is all-embracing — 'Winter kept us warm . . .' It slips into 'Summer surprised us . . .' and 'we stopped in the colonnade . . .' and then, without dramatic differentiation, into the specifically female 'I' of the Marie episode. It is 'I' whose thoughts and feelings are charted through the poem:

> I had not thought death had undone so many    (l.63)
> I think we are in rats' alley    (l.115)
> I sat down and wept    (l.182)
> At my back, in a cold blast, I hear    (l.185)
> We who were living are now dying    (l.329)
> Shall I at least set my lands in order?    (l.425)

Eliot's voice is deliberately not private and individual; he borrows the voices of others — Dante, Baudelaire, Spenser, Verlaine, Ezekiel, Shakespeare, St Augustine, Marvell and many more. His borrowed voices are not necessarily male (they include the woman poet, Sappho); it is not their gender but their role as prophets and poets that is significant. However, female prophets and poets — at least, those whose voices have been recorded in writing for posterity — have been a tiny minority, so the 'I' that is an amalgamation and distillation of all the voices of Eliot's reading will, inevitably, seem essentially male. A feminist reading might well accuse *The Waste Land* of too easily categorising women as creatures to pity, scorn or patronise. A female reader can feel at one with Eliot's 'I' and can share the vision of *The Waste Land* only if she responds comfortably from within the male-dominated culture which produced both the poet and his poem.

# AFTERTHOUGHTS

### 1

What do you understand by Saunders's claim that Madame Sosostris is 'a device rather than a character' (page 49)?

### 2

Do you think that 'In the Cage' (see page 50) might have been a better title for the second section of *The Waste Land*?

### 3

This essay draws on biographical information about Eliot's life in considering his presentation of women. How justified is this?

### 4

Consider the implications of the last two sentences of this essay. Is *The Waste Land* a sexist poem in your view?

**Christopher Mills**

*Christopher Mills is Head of English at Larkmead School in Abingdon, and author of several critical studies.*

ESSAY

# The unity of *The Waste Land*

*The Waste Land* seems obscure at first because the chronological logic of a story is replaced by a sequence of images that follows an imaginative logic and omits explanatory, connecting matter. This is partly the result of extensive cutting, for in its first draft the poem was very long and rambling. Eliot's friend, the poet Ezra Pound, reduced the text to its bare essentials and Eliot approved. Hence the dedication:

> For Ezra Pound
> *il miglior fabbro* [the greater craftsman].

Pound's cutting left such large imaginative leaps in the text, however, that some critics saw the work only as a collection of separate poems. My purpose in this essay is to suggest that it is, in fact, a unified whole.

The poem is unified by the sequence of images, each enlarged by echoes and recurring symbols from previous sections, which build towards the final effect; by the journey in each section and our pilgrimage through the waste land, which will eventually lead to an understanding of it and the possibility of renewal; by the motif of searching for a lost father, a guiding force, ultimately found in God; and perhaps by the figure of

Tiresias, who eventually incorporates all the characters, allowing us to recognise everyman in each. The poem is in fact structured through its echoes — the repeated ideas and analogies that reappear in each section — which is precisely the structure of Buddha's Fire Sermon. Ultimately, the reader senses the cumulative effect of the poem's separate but related pictures. They suggest man's degeneracy, particularly his degenerate love, the only cure for which will be divine love.

The title of section I, taken from the Anglican funeral service, suggests a ritual of dust thrown — 'ashes to ashes, dust to dust' — echoed in 'stony rubbish' (l.20) and 'a handful of dust' (l.30), and the rebirth of the soul after the death of the body, echoed in the sprouting corpse (ll.71–72). It starts, however, by rejecting Chaucer's opening to *The Canterbury Tales*. Chaucer's spring prompts the positive aspects of secular and spiritual love as folk 'longen . . . to goon on pilgrimages' and his nightingale sings of love, unlike Philomel in sections II and III of *The Waste Land*. Here, 'the cruellest month', spring denies nature, and is painful because a desert is stirred to life after the forgetfulness of snow.

Like the fragments at the end, the opening lines summarise some of the poem's ideas: the mixing of 'Memory and desire' (l.3) which produces the pictures of the poem; the denial of nature and love that causes the waste land; forgetfulness and burial, a retreat from reality; the painful start to the pilgrimage we must make. Indeed, all the themes of section I are echoed throughout the poem, suggesting negative aspects of life and death: winter preferred to spring; memory to life; barren love; people 'neither/ Living nor dead' (ll.39–40); 'death had undone so many' (l.63) in the picture of the crowd in the 'Unreal City' who are the living dead of Dante's Purgatory; the corpse, the dead past that cannot remain buried because it will resprout with April; and the sense that all men are the same: 'You! hypocrite lecteur! — mon semblable, — mon frère!' (l.76)

Marie is the first character we meet. The German form of her name would normally be Maria and her insistence upon being German suggests that perhaps, like others, she represents the displaced person, separated from her Russian roots (possibly because of territorial divisions after the First World War) and denying her heritage:

Bin gar keine Russin, stamm' aus Litauen, echt deutsch.

(l.12)

[I am not Russian, I come from Lithuania, pure German.]

She introduces the lost father theme because, apart from possibly denying her roots, her childhood memories are of her cousin, not her father. The good parts of her memory, the feeling of freedom in the mountains, are now lost to her because her life has become a retreat:

I read half the night and go south in the winter.

(l.18)

She is bound, like the rich woman of section II, by the social calendar, not the natural seasons.

This begins the journey motif. In the Grail legend, the Fisher King loses his virility through sexual mutilation or illness and his property becomes a waste land because — in Vegetation myths — fruitfulness depends upon the King's virility. His lands can only be restored to fertility if someone goes on a quest to find the reason for his afflictions. The quester journeys to the Grail chapel and undergoes trials to discover the Grail's purpose and interpret its symbols. Eliot uses the idea of the tortured king, the waste land and the quester's journey and trials, extending the symbolism to articulate a vision of spiritual and physical decay. In each section of the poem, inhabitants of the waste land are journeying: through routines of a social world in the first three, through the purifying sea in section IV and through a nightmarish spiritual fantasy in section V, which probes the true situation which these social routines and a failure to grasp experience have hidden. Thus Marie has wasted her potential and the tragedy of this and the hyacinth girl picture is that both suggest beauty but it is buried in the waste land, the description of which in section I already has a hint of the nightmare of section V where we shall be shown 'fear in a handful of dust' (l.30):

What are the roots that clutch, what branches grow
Out of this stony rubbish? Son of man,
You cannot say, or guess, for you know only
A heap of broken images, where the sun beats,
And the dead tree gives no shelter, the cricket no relief,

And the dry stone no sound of water. . . .

(ll.19–24)

The hyacinth girl picture is similarly one of wasted potential, the first of the portrayals of a barren experience of love. Here, the waste is caused by the man's inability to express his feelings since, living in a waste land, he is no more alive than Marie or the characters of later sections:

> . . . I could not
> Speak, and my eyes failed, I was neither
> Living nor dead . . .

(ll.38–40)

The episode is enveloped by two quotations from Wagner's opera of tragic love, *Tristan und Isolde*. Here, the first is the song of the homeward-bound sailor, the second, '*Oed' und leer das Meer*' (l.42 — 'The sea is empty and barren'), an image of the desolation in the man's vision into 'the heart of light' (l.41). The reference to the song again links forward, however, to section III, where the typist's seduction occurs 'at the voilet hour, the evening hour' that 'brings the sailor home from sea' (ll.220–201).

These pictures begin the sequence of images that will build towards the final effect in the poem and the important recurring symbols also appear in this first section, in Madame Sososstris's Tarot symbols: the sailor, the wheel, the one-eyed merchant, the Hanged Man, Death by Water, 'crowds of people, walking round in a ring' (l.56) are all echoed later. The sailor is also the one-eyed merchant of Smyrna, Mr Eugenides, in section III, later drowned as the Phoenician sailor in section IV. The wheel also appears in section IV as a warning to those who, like Phlebas, try to direct their own destiny (though Phlebas's body was at least destroyed by life-giving water whilst his spirit gained peace, in contrast to those who still live paltry lives in the waste land). The Hanged Man reappears in section V (ll.362–363) and the 'crowds of people' who inhabit the 'Unreal City' of sections I and III are swarming 'hordes' in section V. As we move through the poem, all these ideas from section I will be echoed, for each picture in the poem both stands on its own and becomes a part of a unified whole, gathering ultimately in a nightmarish confusion before order is restored through understanding.

'The Game of Chess' of section II is thus another view of degenerate love. The description at the start, of the woman's surroundings — she is the Queen of the chess set — also parodies the passion of another queen, Cleopatra. The opening line misquotes Enobarbus's description of the truly royal lover in Shakespeare's *Antony and Cleopatra*, 'The barge she sat in, like a burnish'd throne' (II.2.199). Also, in Middleton's play, *Women Beware Women*, the characters pretend to be playing a game of chess in order to distract attention from an attempt at seduction. The anticipation is suggested here in 'Pressing lidless eyes and waiting for a knock upon the door' (l.138). And the woman, bored in her lavish surroundings and by the social routine:

> The hot water at ten.
> And, if it rains, a closed car at four.
>
> (l.134–135)

accepts that 'we shall play a game of chess' (l.137). Decay is suggested in the archaic diction of the opening scene that describes the list of unnatural items: 'fruited vines' are 'wrought', the Cupidan 'golden', light comes from candelabra, 'sevenbranched' as in a church but used for no religious purpose, the dolphin is 'carvèd', swimming in a 'sad light' and 'the sylvan scene' is only a painting, one of several 'withered stumps of time', telling a story of denial and violation that cannot be explained because the bird can only sing 'Jug Jug', just as later, the mad Ophelia, rejected by Hamlet whom she loved and who had killed her father, cannot articulate her woes. The last line of this section quotes her final confused words: 'Good night, ladies, good night, sweet ladies, good night, good night' (l.172). It is of course an ironic rejoinder to the preceding 'goonight' (l.170–171). The meaninglessness of this social world and the purposelessness of section II's journey:

> I shall rush out as I am, and walk the street
> With my hair down, so. What shall we do tomorrow?
>
> (ll.132–133)

is emphasised by a preoccupation with burial ('Where the dead men lost their bones', l.116), by their deliberately protecting themselves from the life-giving rain ('And if it rains, a closed car') and because their sexual union is only an escape from boredom into momentary pleasure, avoiding procreation. In contrast to Cleopatra's, this is a world of sterility.

What mainly differentiates the two couples pictured in this section is social class. In the game of chess we have moved from the Queen to the Pawns, but find them similarly denying nature, interested in false teeth and chemicals (though for abortions rather than make-up), squandering Albert's money as the Queen of the section has squandered hers on scents and jewels, and Lil looking as 'antique' (l.156) as the other's collection. Their fertility only results from Albert's inability to leave Lil alone for they too want to avoid children, indeed, deliberately reject new life:

It's them pills I took, to bring it off, she said.

(1.159)

The cockney woman's question at the end of the speech:

What you get married for if you don't want children?

(1.164)

is clearly a reflection on both couples.

In these distorted relationships, opportunities for fatherhood are rejected. The theme of the lost father, hinted at in section I is thus expanded upon and, here, is further suggested by the analogies: echoes of original sin and the loss of a spiritual father by Adam and Eve; of *The Tempest* ('Those are pearls that were his eyes' (l.126)) and Ferdinand's drowned father; and the closing words from Ophelia's first mad speech reminding us that both she and Hamlet had lost their fathers. The inadequacy of earthly love is also being suggested, for Ophelia is another forsaken lover like Isolde and Philomel. These themes link clearly to the final section and redemption by divine love, and a sense of urgency is created by:

HURRY UP PLEASE IT'S TIME

which tolls for the burial of the dead and urges the inhabitants of the Waste Land to redeem this time, at present 'withered stumps', so that fertility can return.

The journeys and loves presented in section III are equally

fruitless. We are taken on a hopeless, aimless journey past the deserted Thames, through noisy streets to Mrs Porter, through the City to a homosexual invitation to the Metropole or through the mechanical world to the bored mechanical typist: again, all images of distorted sexuality with no procreative purpose. The Thames waters are 'the waters of Leman' (l.182), a medieval word for lover, the nymphs' friends 'the loitering heirs of city directors' who have departed and 'left no addresses' (ll.180–181) to avoid the responsibilities of pregnancy, Spenser's river has become a 'dull canal' (l.189). The Psalmist ('By the waters of Babylon we sat down and wept' — Psalm 137) wept on being led in captivity from the holy city of Jerusalem; here, we weep at the decay.

The lines:

> But at my back in a cold blast I hear
> The rattle of bones . . .

(ll.185–186)

are an allusion to Marvell's 'To His Coy Mistress', where the poet insists that his mistress should make love before time hurries them to the grave ('But at my back I alwaies hear/ Times winged Charriot hurrying near') because time causes decay rather than growth; and the lines:

> But at my back from time to time I hear
> The sound of horns and motors . . .

(ll.196–197)

allude to Day's 'Parliament of Bees', where the 'noise of horns and hunting' bring Actaeon to Diana and love is a diverting pastime. These allusions remind us that love is now either a kind of death or treated as a plaything to divert the mind from substantial matters and they pick up the sense of urgency created in section II by 'HURRY UP PLEASE IT'S TIME'.

The effect of this waste land on individuals is first seen as Sweeney, Eliot's figure of the barbaric man, goes to Mrs Porter, the brothel keeper of a song, parodied in:

> O the moon shone bright on Mrs Porter
> And on her daughter

(ll.199–200)

Although he goes 'in the spring' (l.198), the Waste Land spring, as in section I, is barren and the suggestion of the innocence of baptism in the foot-washing and children singing is immediately betrayed by the echo from section II of distorted sexuality in the 'Twit twit twit' (l.203) of the bird and the memory of Philomel's violation.

Elizabeth too (l.279), the queen of this section, is a symbol of sterility. Her magnificent but pointless journey contrasts with the drabness of the modern-day Thames pictured in the parodied Spenserian song ('The river sweats' — l.266) and with Cleopatra's journey to Antony, for Elizabeth's relationship with Leicester was fruitless. She is closer to the Queen of the chess set in section II. Thus both passages here end with the sighs of Wagner's song and are followed by the confessions of the three Thames-daughters, each seduction of whom is another image of sterility, violation and forsaken love.

Despite their apparent individuality, the figures in section III are representative of all mankind. So, we now realise, were those of the previous sections. The characters are brought together by the unifying figure of Tiresias, representing both sexes and having seen it all before. He witnesses the typist's return to her waste land and knows what will follow:

> I Tiresias, old man with wrinkled dugs
> Perceived the scene, and foretold the rest —
>
> . . .
>
> And I, Tiresias, have foresuffered all
> Enacted on this same divan or bed

(ll.228–229; 243–244)

The moral context is suggested by the rhythmically serious alternately rhymed pentameters in contrast to the tired mechanical scene.

As the 'I' of the poem that he has now become, Tiresias utters the fragments from Augustine and the Fire Sermon at the end, denouncing the sterile burning of lust but also articulating a desire for salvation:

> O Lord Thou pluckest me out

(l.309)

For whilst, in section III, the confessions of the Thames-daughters conclude our journey through the social waste land, the final stage of the pilgrimage is also suggested by the recurring theme of the lost father. The reference is again to Ferdinand in *The Tempest*, who found his father, Alonso — whom he had imagined had died in a shipwreck — safe and well at the end; Prospero, whose place was usurped by his brother Antonio, is also restored. Thus the lines:

> Musing upon the king, my brother's wreck
> And on the king my father's death before him
>
> (ll.191–192)

suggest the one lost father who was found again, the king restored to a kingdom that would flourish anew. Also, in the Grail legend, the ritual feet-washing is accompanied by singing children and is a prelude to the Fisher King's recovery. Section III therefore suggests hope.

Section IV offers the quester one possible answer: spiritual rebirth through sacrifice of the body as the fires of lust and sterility are put out with life-giving water. For the merchant, now transfigured into Phlebas, the burdens of worldly diversions ('profit and loss') are lifted, following the kind of sacrifice everyone must be prepared to make if rebirth is to be possible. It is also, like fire, one of the trials of the quester's journey. However, 'the wheel' (1.320) must be guided by the proper hand and man — since Phlebas stands for us all — may need a higher authority to direct his destiny: 'Consider Phlebas, who was once handsome and tall as you.' (1.321)

Section V remains in this visionary world, picturing a nightmarish waste land, created by the inhabitants of the physical social world. With social rites and diversions burnt away, the images suggest the reality of man's condition, echoing those from section I, in order to show 'fear in a handful of dust' (1.30). The unreality of the City in section I has now become an affliction of the whole world of the earlier sections:

> Jerusalem Athens Alexandria
> Vienna London
> Unreal
>
> (ll.374–376)

and images from the rest of the poem — 'hooded hordes',

'cracked earth', 'violet air', 'falling towers', 'bats with baby faces', 'towers upside down' — are brought together in a disconnected nightmare, the sense of which is enhanced by the variations in line length and the lack of punctuation. Only rain, 'buried' as we saw in section I by Marie and the hyacinth girl, can give these broken images new order.

Having now journeyed through the waste land, we know that rain, symbolising rebirth and renewal, is the purpose of the pilgrimage. It has not come yet:

> Here is no water but only rock

(1.331)

but it is constantly anticipated by the word 'if' (ll.335, 338, 345, 347–348, 352), and the verse creates a rhythmic panting effect in the shortened lines:

> If there were water
> And no rock
> If there were rock
> And also water

(ll.345–348)

We even hallucinate over its appearance, 'drip drop drip drop . . ./ But there is no water' (ll.357–358). Thunder rolls, the cock crows, lightning flashes and:

> . . . a damp gust
> Bringing rain

(ll.393–394)

is felt, but we are told:

> . . . the limp leaves
> Waited for rain . . .

(ll.395–396)

No rain falls. It cannot, because no one is yet prepared to make the proper sacrifice and no one can control the wheel. The plain is still 'arid' at the end. Though the pilgrimage is over, the chapel is 'an empty chapel, only the wind's home' (1.388) because the father is lost and there is no controlling force to guide:

> . . . those hooded hordes swarming

Over endless plains, stumbling in cracked earth

(ll.368–369)

The possibility of renewal is suggested in the opening by the reference to Gethsemane and Golgotha, 'the agony in stony places' (l.324) and:

> . . . thunder of spring over distant mountains
> He who was living is now dead
> We who were living are now dying
> With a little patience

(ll.327–330)

Provided, like Christ, we make the necessary sacrifice then rebirth with spring rain is possible. So there is still hope and Christ appears with the narrator as the Hanged Man, a protective angel, even though he is not yet seen clearly:

> There is always another one walking beside you
> Gliding wrapt in a brown mantle, hooded

(ll.362–363)

The passage reminds us of the two disciples walking to Emmaus after the crucifixion, unaware of Christ's resurrection, glimpsing a third person who disappears when they turn round. Christ has appeared here as a symbol of the possibility of redemption.

Hope lies in obeying the thunder's voice. We must give, 'Datta', not the material contents of wills, 'under seals broken by the lean solicitor' (l.408); we must surrender our hearts. We must sympathise, 'Dayadhvam', leaving the prisons of our self-obsession, giving to the community, reviving 'a broken Coriolanus' who failed to give and sympathise and cut himself off from the community. Finally we must submit to control, 'Damyata', so that the wheel may be properly steered and the heart beat 'obedient' to the 'controlling hands' of God. Although we have not submitted yet — the 'heart *would have* responded' (l.420 — my italics) — we have learnt what must be done.

We therefore return to the physical world and the repeated image of fishing (connected to fertility rituals in Buddhist belief too) with a new understanding, knowing what before we had buried. We have explored the waste land to its core and know what must be done if it is to become fertile again, so we can sit 'with the arid plain behind' (1.424). Nothing can revitalise it until the proper sacrifice has been made but we can begin:

'Shall I at least set my lands in order?'

(1.425)

London Bridge, where 'a crowd flowed' in section I, is 'falling down'. Let it. Consider what can be done.

The final fragments suggest purification of lust by fire as in section III:

*Poi s'ascose nel foco che gli affina*
[He disappeared into the purifying flame]

but Dante's spirits welcomed this punishment because it was not hopeless or eternal, so the next line asks, 'When shall I be free like the swallow?':

*Quando fiam uti chelidon* — O swallow swallow

perhaps faintly echoing Philomel but also Marie who fled the freedom of the mountains to migrate south.

*Le Prince d'Aquitaine à la tour abolie*

from the poem 'The Disinherited' by Gerard de Nerval, suggests the 'empty chapel' at the end of the pilgrimage. Thus these fragments bring together major ideas from the whole poem. The final allusion is to Hieronymo whose feigned madness in Kyd's *Spanish Tragedy* recalls Hamlet and Ophelia from section II and the ultimate sacrifice of himself. For what is demanded is the sacrifice of the self or, in contrast to the degraded forms of love offered in sections I–III, love which is giving, sympathetic and 'obedient to controlling hands'; that is, divine love. We shall then have found the father and attain the final blessing: 'Shantih shantih shantih'. Like the ending of section III, these words combine the Christian and Buddhist philosophies, for they are both the formal ending to an Upanishad, an ancient Indian philosophical scriptural treatise and the final blessing in the Protestant Communion:

The peace of God, which passeth all understanding,
Keep your hearts and minds in the knowledge and love of God.

To see *The Waste Land*, therefore, as a collection of separate poems is to misunderstand its structure. The images, analogies and symbols of the opening are echoed in each section; recurring images of the social and spiritual desert are especially obvious in the first and last sections, binding the two together; Tiresias provides unity by making us see each specific example in the poem as only representative of its type; and above all, perhaps, the search for the father, the journey framework and the concern with love — first in its degraded form, ultimately, with the insight gained from the pilgrimage, in its supreme form — gives the poem a unity which we cannot avoid sensing at the end. There may be no chronological progression but there is a structural logic representing a spiritual progression, a spiritual pilgrimage through the waste land of society and the inner self which the cumulative effect of the poem's pictures and echoes has suggested. At journey's end, we may appear still to be back where we started but the experience has led us to understand the 'heap of broken images' (1.22) that we met at the start and with that wisdom, we can, if we will, set our lands in order, make them fertile again and find 'the peace which passeth all understanding'.

# AFTERTHOUGHTS

## 1

What do you make of Mills's distinction between 'chronological logic' and 'imaginative logic' (see opening sentence)?

## 2

Given the extent of Pound's cutting (page 59), is it reasonable to describe *The Waste Land* as Eliot's poem?

## 3

Consider the lost father motif identified in this essay. How significant do you find it?

## 4

Discuss the differences between Mill's interpretation of rain in *The Waste Land* (pages 68–69) and the views expressed by Pinkney (pages 27–29).

**Sam S Baskett**

*Sam Baskett is Professor of English at Michigan State University, USA, and author of numerous critical studies.*

ESSAY

# Eliot's London

Born in St Louis, Missouri, a hundred miles or so from the birth-place of the quintessentially American Mark Twain, T S Eliot thus grew up as a 'South Westerner'. He was nonetheless always aware of the geographical and cultural New England heritage of the Eliot and other related families: his Calvinist Eliot ancestor had migrated from East Coker, Somerset, to Massachusetts in the seventeenth century. In 1953, Eliot, by then a Nobel laureate and a British citizen for twenty-five years, described his 'personal landscape' as a composite of the 'seedily drably urban' imagery of St Louis, where 'the Mississippi was the most powerful feature of nature', and of his 'emotionally charged' country landscape of coastal New England, which he knew through summer residence and years of schooling in that region. Eliot's persistent, ambivalent identification with these quite different areas was to be repeated in transatlantic terms, for however vividly formative his American images, he chose to live almost his entire adult life in London. On one level he could jest equivocally, when asked whether he was an American or English poet, that whichever Auden was, he was the other. But Eliot's individualistic expatriation, his search for a congenial geographical/cultural location in which to ground his identity, had far more profound reverberations. A quest for transcendent meaning related to place was the controlling impulse of Eliot's life and work.

In August 1914, having completed three years of graduate work in philosophy at Harvard University, Eliot arrived in London for his first extended stay, taking up lodgings at 28 Bedford Place. His initial reactions were negative — he did not feel at home — but his meeting with his fellow countryman Ezra Pound was momentous. Eliot read 'The Love Song of J. Alfred Prufrock' to him in September. Immediately recognising its merit, Pound set about building Eliot's reputation, securing the publication of the poem in America in the June 1915 issue of *Poetry*. Eliot had come to England on a Harvard Fellowship to continue his philosophical studies at Oxford, which he did during the Michaelmas 1914 term, but not before Pound had introduced him to several American writers living in London and to Wystan Lewis, who published 'Preludes' and 'Rhapsody on a Windy Night' in the avant-garde literary journal *Blast* for July 1915. Lewis's impression of the poet is striking, anticipating some of the qualities to be discerned in later portraits of Eliot by the artist: a 'sleek, tall, attractive, transatlantic apparition — with a sort of Giocondo smile, *moqueur* to the marrow . . .'

Although Eliot spent two terms at Oxford, increasingly he was disenchanted both with the place and with philosophical studies, for whatever complex of reasons. In any event, he was back in London in June 1915, and late that month he married Vivien Haigh-Wood, whom he had met sometime during the previous months. Radically unsuited for each other, they both endured years of unhappiness together until Eliot forced a separation in 1932. His family reacted strongly to the sudden marriage, and despite his hurried trip back home to secure their approval, their disappointment in a son whom they had expected to pursue a career in philosophy at Harvard made a permanent impact on him. Having given up his fellowship, it was now necessary for Eliot to make a living, and he took a position at High Wycombe Grammar School in Buckinghamshire for autumn 1915, then moving after one unsatisfactory term to Highgate Junior School in London, where he taught for a year. Among his pupils was John Betjeman, who remembered the 'American master' as 'a remote, quiet figure'.

It is not clear at what point Eliot considered himself permanently settled in London, but when he completed his dissertation on F H Bradley in 1917 he did not consider returning to teach at Harvard. Disliking grammar school teaching, he secured a position as clerk in the Colonial and Foreign Department at Lloyds at 17 Cornhill. Despite finding the work wearing, he seems to have been a success — in retrospect, one of his superiors thought if he had stayed at Lloyds eventually he would have made a good branch manager — and at least the position gave him more time for writing than did school teaching. In 1925, he obtained a congenial position as a director of the publishing firm of Faber and Gwyer in Russell Square, a post he retained for the rest of his life. Ironically, one of the most private of individuals — personally shy, even often unsure and tormented — had a public career as a successful London businessman.

As Eliot's letters frequently attest, he did not find his London life dull, despite his continuing complaints about problems both at home and at the office. Much of the interest must have come from his increasing reputation in the literary world following the publication of *Prufrock and Other Observations* (1917) and *Poems* (1920). He had also begun to establish himself as a critic: the first collection of essays, *The Sacred Wood*, appeared in 1920. With the publication of *The Waste Land* in 1922, he was moving toward the status he was to hold for the next two decades as the most influential poet and critic writing in English, the pre-eminent man of letters in what has been called 'The Age of Eliot'. Self-consciously committing himself to this life and to the whole of English civilisation, including the formal adoption of Anglican orthodoxy, Eliot to his English friends nonetheless remained very much an American as Eliot himself admitted in print. In 1945, writing in a British periodical he signed himself *métoikos*, Greek for 'resident alien'.

Fragments of Eliot's life in London are represented in his poetry in graphic geographical detail. As Sir John Betjeman observed, he is 'a poet of London', especially in *The Waste Land*, sensitive to the atmosphere of the place and recording his impressions in strikingly realistic images, however 'unreal' his surroundings may seem to the quester in his various guises. At the end of the first almost photographic passage describing the daily influx of the business crowd streaming into the City (ll.60–68), Eliot's note wrily comments, 'A phenomenon which I have often noticed'. One may check the literal accuracy of the description in two ways: Eliot's lines echo in the reader's mind as he moves with the 'crowd flow[ing] over London Bridge/ . . . up the hill and down King William Street,/ To where St Mary Woolnoth keep[s] the hours'. The fog of a winter dawn, however, is no longer 'brown', contemporary pollution being provided by carbon monoxide rather than low-grade coal fires. The swarming scene and the umbrellas and briefcases of the black-clad hordes indeed make it necessary that 'each man [fix] his eyes before his feet'. Now that the Saint Mary Woolnoth clock is repaired after many years, one may even experience the 'phenomenon' of 'a dead sound on the final stroke of nine' as did Eliot for many years as he emerged from the Bank Station, having taken the Underground from his flat in Clarence Gardens, and proceeded to his desk at Lloyds a few yards away. Or one may corroborate the representational accuracy of the lines by taking the standard tourist bus tour along the Strand through the business district and hear the guide, admitting to no inkling of the poet, droningly call off all of the place names from 'The Burial of the Dead' and 'The Fire Sermon' (ll.60–68, 258–265). This is the world experienced by Eliot, the businessman, at rush hour each work-day morning for many years. The explicit geography thus serves as a strikingly real setting for a poem which also explores other dimensions of reality. Some of the references are perhaps less immediately obvious than those just cited. In 'The Fire Sermon', now 'Under the brown fog of a winter noon', there is a reference to 'Mr Eugenides, the Smyrna merchant/ Unshaven, with a pocket full of currants/ C.i.f. London: documents at sight'. (See ll.208–211.) In an explanatory note to line 210, one of the Notes often regarded as inconsequential 'filler', Eliot prosaically but not irrelevantly explains, 'The currants were quoted at a price "cost insurance and freight to London"; and the Bill of Lading, etc., were to be handed to the buyer upon payment of the sight draft'. A two-minute walk from Lloyds was, and is, the Jamaica Wine House, established in 1869, so a plaque on the building attests, but the site of a coffee shop set up in the seventeenth century by a Greek brought to England to brew morning coffee for a merchant, who had acquired the taste while in Smyrna. The shop became noted down through the decades as a place where merchants and insurance brokers transacted business. It seems likely that Eliot had pub lunches at the

Jamaica, but in any event its history informs several lines of his poems, suggesting a geographical thread as a base of what might seem random juxtaposition.

Another cluster of place references is even more evocative. After the episode, 'foresuffered' by Tiresias, between the typist and the 'small house agent's clerk', the quester hears 'Beside a public bar in Lower Thames Street,/ The pleasant whining of a mandoline/ And a clatter and a chatter from within/ Where fishmen lounge at noon: where the walls/ Of Magnus Martyr hold/ Inexplicable splendour of Ionian white and gold' (ll.260–265). Eliot's note to line 264 perhaps points to a distinction he made between St Mary Woolnoth, 'the banker's church' as it is sometimes called, sitting directly above Bank Station, and St Magnus Martyr: 'The interior of [the latter] is to my mind one of the finest among Wren's interiors'. In 1921 Eliot wrote of the peace to be found by 'the solitary visitor' in the churches of the City, in contrast to 'the dust and tumult' outside. A few yards down Lower Thames Street is the site of the Billingsgate Fish Market and St Magnus Martyr has been identified as the fishmen's church, the Worshipful Company of Fishmongers even presenting wooden benches to the church courtyard in observance of the coronation of Elizabeth II. Across the street is The Walrus and the Carpenter, formerly The Cock until the late 1970s, a pub catering to fishmen's special hours as the lines quoted and a sign still in evidence in 1979 made clear: 'The Cock: We respectfully remind our Customers that only those engaged on Business in Billingsgate Market are permitted to be served with alcoholic refreshment before 11:30 a.m.' The 'meaning' of this complex passage is not defined by its sharply outlined geographical setting, but it is inextricably bound up with it.

Many other geographic sites in the London area are mentioned in 'The Fire Sermon' — the Thames, Greenwich reach, the Isle of Dogs, Highbury, Richmond, Kew, Moorgate — providing a backdrop for the quester's multiple voice, but one particular reference requires some explication, the title of the section itself. A few yards up Fish Street Hill from St Magnus Martyr is the Monument commemorating the Great Fire of London, which destroyed much of the area in 1666. The inscription on the base of the Monument, after noting many physical details of the fire, concludes, 'On the third day, when it had now altogether vanished all human counsel and resources, at the bidding, as we may well believe of Heaven, the fatal fire stayed its course and everywhere died out'. This capsule fire sermon points thus to both the geographic and transcendent significances implicit in the Monument — and in the title of this section of *The Waste Land*.

Although London remained his home for the rest of his life, Eliot did not again focus so directly and extensively on London scenes that any particular work could be considered a 'London poem', as, in some respects, *The Waste Land* surely is. In this poem the reader comes to 'know' some bits of London better from having read Eliot. But the significant facts are not just that he lived and worked in London, that the city inevitably shaped his attitudes and personality. The poem is the thing; and ultimately Eliot's London is what he made of it in his poetry. It has been observed that there are essentially three attitudes that a lyric poet can take towards the description of place: the poet can use it as an external backdrop to his thinking; he can transform the place into his mind; or he can attempt to make a place of the poem itself. Eliot's rendering of London in his poetry is, among other things, a composite of these orientations toward descriptions of place.

As we have seen, realistically described London scenes serve as a modern urban background from which the quester feels largely alienated, but which, if he is to be a 'modern' poet of the city he must enter — the alternative being the death in life which has 'undone so many'. He wanders through the streets as a spectator, as the note to line 218 expressly emphasises: 'Tiresias, although a mere spectator and not indeed a "character", is yet the most important personage in the poem, uniting all the rest'. Locked in the tower of his solipsism, the spectator can only observe; and he is doubly disadvantaged — he finds the external place a death in life, insufficient, 'unreal'. Yet his emotional distance permits him to see this external world clearly and to describe its 'unreality' in graphic detail in Eliot's own adaptation of eighteenth-century topographical poetry of place.

Viewing such an external place, however, the poet has other resources: the capacity to transform the external scene into the poet's mind. It is immediately apparent that the graphic scenes of London tend to blur into other places and other times. A crowd flows over London Bridge provoking a gasp of realistic recognition; but the allusions to and echoes of other eras, reinforced by Eliot's pointed Notes, make the reader aware that Eliot has transformed the City into Baudelaire's Paris, Dante's *Inferno*, the worlds of the Grail legend and *The Golden Bough*. Starkly solid in the 1920s, London Bridge is 'falling down' along with other 'Falling towers/ Jerusalem Athens Alexandria/ Vienna London/ Unreal'. The contemporary river that 'sweats/ Oil and tar' is also the Thames of Spenser's 'Prothalamion' and of the dalliance of Elizabeth and Leicester, as well as evocative of other celebrated waters. The quester enters into the 'Inexplicable splendour of Ionian white and gold' of St Magnus Martyr through what had been the street leading to the previous London Bridge, 1176–1831 — and to a Roman wharf of the first century. The 'fire' symbol evokes the London Great Fire, but also Augustine's 'burning' and Buddha's 'Fire Sermon'. If the quester brings to mind a tormented bank clerk in the early 1920s, he is united, as just noted, in Tiresias with all the other 'spectators' in the poem: 'What Tiresias *sees*, in fact, is the substance of the poem'.

What is seen, of course, is a construct of the imagination, external London extended in time and space as transformed in the poet's mind as he absorbs and becomes a place. Earlier landscape poets, such as Wordsworth, were prone to absorb beneficent nature, usually rural. The created region in the poet's mind tended to be reinforced with literary and religious associations beyond significant topography. Eliot, who once remarked that Wordsworth was the last poet to 'see' nature, does find in his mind 'hints and guesses' of a meaningful place, the hyacinth garden, 'the pleasant whining of a Mandoline', 'What the Thunder said'. And at the end of *The Waste Land* he manages to will a vision continuing the religious and literary associations alluded to throughout as a way, like that followed by many romantic landscape poets who were his predecessors, of transforming the external world into a place in his mind he can inhabit authentically. Fishing for reality while London Bridge is 'falling down', he determines 'at least [to] set my own lands in order', although in his visionary effort, he may seem in a common-sense world 'mad again', like Thomas Kyd's

Hieronymo. Eliot's London topography thus becomes a topography of the inner eye as it is re-created in his imagination. As Stephen Spender has remarked, Eliot saw England — London, tradition — in a distinctly Eliotian-American way, in which contemporary existence is a kind of parenthesis in a past that is not a memory but a force that is as living as the present, an individual 'patria', or true nation, towards which he had been expatriating all along.

It is impossible, of course, to 'know' London, or any other place for that matter, as Eliot's lines all but admit, but he did not cease in his efforts to transform an 'unreal' external world observed by indifferent spectators into something that mattered. In Eliot's poetry, the reader shares a city that is richer and stranger for this transformation.

# AFTERTHOUGHTS

**1**

Do you think that someone who did not know London at all could appreciate *The Waste Land*?

**2**

What examples can you find in the poetry you know of the 'three attitudes that a lyric poet can take towards the description of place' identified in this essay (page 78)?

**3**

What do you understand by 'solipsism' (page 78)?

**4**

What significance does Baskett attach to Eliot's American origins?

**Robert Wilson**

*Robert Wilson teaches English at Merchant Taylors' School. He is the author of a number of school text books and editions, his most recent publication being* Novels *(Longman, 1987).*

ESSAY

# Is there hope in *The Waste Land?*

> April is the cruellest month, breeding
> Lilacs out of the dead land, mixing
> Memory and desire, stirring
> Dull roots with spring rain.

(ll.1–4)

These opening lines describe a reluctant return to living as spring forces movement and growth upon us. They are often contrasted, as Eliot intended them to be, with the opening lines of the General Prologue to Chaucer's *Canterbury Tales*:

> Whan that Aprill with his shoures soote
> The droghte of March hath perced to the roote,
> And bathed every veyne in swich licour
> Of which vertu engendred is the flour . . .

> [When the sweet showers of April have pierced the dryness of March to its root and soaked every vein in moisture whose quickening force brings the flower to birth . . .]

Here is joyful, medieval acclamation of the returning vitality of the season and its fertile powers which leads to a vigorous response to its summons:

Thanne longen folk to goon on pilgrimages,
And palmeres for to seken straunge strondes

[then people long to go on pilgrimages and pious wanderers to
explore foreign lands]

In *The Waste Land*, modern man — spiritually derelict and
alienated from the forces of nature — wishes to remain asleep,
semi-conscious.

All this is true, but it is not all that is to be said. For the
primary emphasis, as in Chaucer's lines, is on the irresistible
urgencies of April. The spring will come whether we like it or
not and, in spite of our resistance, positive growth takes place
both outside and inside us: the lilacs emerge from a land that
cannot, it seems, have been wholly dead and issues of past,
present and future — 'Memory and desire' — are forced upon
us. Notice too the way these lines are constructed: the crucial
words are verbs of change and happening, all placed promi-
nently at the ends of lines and all requiring onward movement
into succeeding lines. No less than five out of the first seven
lines of the poem end in this way and the associations thus
emphasised are those of growth, fostering and change. An inexorable urging is felt.

It is usual to offer a negative reading of *The Waste Land*,
to regard it as a work of profound, almost unrelieved pessimism,
to concentrate on Eliot's analysis of the manifold aspects of
modern man's spiritual sterility. I shall argue that the poem as
a whole, as in its opening lines, moves irresistibly towards
vitality, and that the poem develops *towards* an experience of
release, redemption, restoration and renewal, even though this
experience is not to be achieved and celebrated within the
confines of the poem. Central to tracing this development is an
understanding of the changing and deepening role of a character
in the poem who I shall identify as the principal Narrator. He
is the voice of criticism, the voice that we feel is closest to that
of the poet. In 'The Burial of the Dead', he is superior and
detached in his exposure of the false values of contemporary life;
in 'The Fire Sermon' and 'What the Thunder said' we shall see
how he becomes more fully implicated in the suffering and
alienation he witnesses and comes to perceive other people and
his own role differently. In short, I shall argue that he takes his

own medicine, begins to experience hints of regeneration and, at the last, evolves a definition of the moral task confronting him, and us.

Three characters in 'The Burial of the Dead' — Marie (ll.8–18), the hyacinth girl (ll.31–42) and Madame Sosostris (ll.43–59) — are presented so as to expose and dismiss any lingering hopes of renewal through a cultured aristocracy, through the experience of romantic love and through what is no more than a superstitious version of spirituality. Eliot also identifies a fourth, deadening element in the modern experience:

> Unreal City,
> Under the brown fog of a winter dawn,
> A crowd flowed over London Bridge, so many,
> I had not thought death had undone so many.

(ll.60–63)

The world of work, of commuting to the City, becomes a communal death-in-life. Individuality is obliterated and the members of the crowd are no more than drops of water in a river that 'flowed over London Bridge' as the Thames flows beneath it. This notion of a controlling stream of life over which the individual has no influence is reinforced when 'flowed' is repeated a few lines later. This state is one of semi-consciousness, of only partial and gloomy vision 'Under the brown fog'.

In exposing and dismissing different manifestations of the semi-consciousness of the age, Eliot is exercising the function of the prophet as critic of his society. But another aspect of the prophetic role is the demand for a change of heart, and twice in this section the Narrator issues just such a challenge. In the manner of an Old Testament prophet, he urges us to recognise the spiritual desert around us and to take shelter from the sun in the shade of a rock where he promises an alternative to:

> Your shadow at morning striding behind you
> Or your shadow at evening rising to meet you;
> I will show you fear in a handful of dust.

(ll.28–30)

Here is the first overt statement of the hope that underlies the

whole of *The Waste Land*. The shadow that strides behind
suggests the past, all those established patterns of experience
that determine and limit the present. In the morning it
oppresses and threatens, hunting us out; in the evening we are
still to be confronted by the self, perhaps in reproach, certainly
*before* us, dominating the future. We are circumscribed by
nothing more than a shadowy, unsubstantial sense of self. The
structure of these two lines, both beginning with 'your' and
ending with 'you', enacts this imprisonment, this egocentric and
mechanical inevitability. 'Rising' is a potent word here — one
thinks of Christ 'rising from the dead' — but rebirth, resurrection must be preceded by death, a fearful confrontation with
man's mortality, 'a handful of dust'. That is the only hope.

We may relate the line back to the epigraph, for the Sybil
of Cumae longs for death, and forward to the bizarre challenge
thrust at Stetson, when — in the manner of one who makes a
horticultural enquiry of a colleague — the Narrator asks:

> That corpse you planted last year in your garden,
> Has it begun to sprout? . . .

(ll.71–72)

He mocks the defensive structures with which we seek to keep
at bay any changes in our lives. We bury their disturbing
aspects and refuse to let them affect our superficial conformity
to socially acceptable mediocrity. Sarcastically, the Narrator
warns against allowing any positive instinctual force to
approach our carefully concealed failure and uncover the
evidence that we have murdered our potential for growth:

> Oh keep the Dog far hence, that's friend to men,
> Or with his nails he'll dig it up again!

(ll.74–75)

How oddly the word 'nails' sounds in that line! It recalls things
hard and inexorable; its associations may lead us to the idea of
suffering, to a 'bed of nails' or to the nailing of Christ to the
cross. Certainly, if our suppressed and buried capacity for
sacrificial death and transformation — as opposed to this false
death, this mere matter of concealment — is activated, we shall
suffer: there will be the pain of the nails in our growth.

Through all this trenchant analysis of the superficiality of our age, the Narrator has remained detached, the critic of society, who rises to the level of sarcastic superiority in his challenge to Stetson. Only in the final line, in the last four words of this section, is a new note sounded:

> You! hypocrite lecteur! — mon semblable, — mon frère!

The denunciation of Stetson includes the reader and the Narrator himself — first as fellow-man, then, more intimately, as brother. Whether they are uttered in scathing loathing or in sad recognition, these words signify a personal identification with the challenge to change. The prophet is implicated in his own criticism.

As the poem develops, we are shown other scenes of emotional and spiritual impoverishment. Increasingly the Narrator is present, shouldering a personal responsibility and participating in the rhythm of death and rebirth which is the poem's acknowledged context. It is this assumption of responsibility which leads us into a hope, an expectation of change. It has begun in the last four words of 'The Burial of the Dead'; it is evident in the broken monologue of the male 'lover' in the first episode of 'A Game of Chess', where he passively suffers the burden of a hysterically demanding woman. But it is in the third section, 'The Fire Sermon', that the Narrator takes on a more central, archetypal role.

At the start of 'The Fire Sermon', he places himself in the scene primarily as an observer, but also as suffering and participating:

> By the waters of Leman I sat down and wept . . .
>
> (1.182)

The line significantly modifies the first verse of Psalm 137:

> By the waters of Babylon, there we sat down, yea, we wept,
> when we remembered Zion.

The exiled Israelites lament the loss of their homeland but Eliot renders the note of mourning in more specific, individual terms. (It may be remarked that he wrote part of *The Waste Land* when receiving treatment for nervous disorders near Lake Leman in Switzerland.) The Narrator's experience of alienation is developed a few lines later:

> . . . I was fishing in the dull canal
> On a winter evening round behind the gashouse
> Musing upon the king my brother's wreck
> And on the king my father's death before him.
>
> (ll.189–192)

In his Notes, Eliot implies that we are to identify the Narrator here with two figures, the Fisher King of Arthurian legends and Ferdinand in *The Tempest*, and, at once, a complex involvement is established. On the one hand, the Fisher King was ruler of a wasted land whose sterility has been caused by his own deep physical and psychic wound. On the other hand, Ferdinand, far from being the *source* of sterility or in any way implicated in evil, signifies youth, vitality and capacity for loving. He and his father, the King of Naples, have been shipwrecked on an island which has been inhabited for twelve years by Prospero, the rightful — but wrongly deposed and exiled — Duke of Milan and his daughter Miranda. Ferdinand and Miranda create a union that will unite the kingdom of Naples with the dukedom of Milan and restore a harmony that an older generation had destroyed. A profound ambivalence is established here: the Narrator identifies himself simultaneously with the roles of suffering sinner and bringer of renewal, with cause and cure. And there is something else here that is, as yet, unresolved: Ferdinand mourns only for his father, who he presumes to have drowned:

> . . . Sitting on a bank,
> Weeping again the King my father's wrack,
> This music crept by me upon the waters.
>
> (*The Tempest* I.2.390–392)

The Narrator, however, contemplates the wreck of his brother, his contemporary ('. . . — mon semblable, — mon frère!') as well as the loss of the tradition, the father. There seems a bemused uncertainty of role, as if the responsibility of kingship has not yet devolved upon the speaker. In his hesitation and anguish, it seems more relevant to connect the Narrator with Hamlet than with Ferdinand, and, indeed, there is a distant echo of *Hamlet* I.2.192: 'The King my father!'

This hesitation, this uncertainty in the role of the Narrator seems resolved some sixty-five lines later in 'The Fire Sermon' when Eliot returns to the same moment from *The Tempest*. The return is effected through a direct quotation, acknowledged as such by being placed within inverted commas. It completes the reference made earlier and it ushers in a passage of positive images and restorative harmonies, projecting into the very heart of the poem a warm anticipation of renewal. Here is the whole passage:

> 'This music crept by me upon the waters'
> And along the Strand, up Queen Victoria Street.
> O City city, I can sometimes hear
> Beside a public bar in Lower Thames Street,
> The pleasant whining of a mandoline
> And a clatter and a chatter from within
> Where fishmen lounge at noon: where the walls
> Of Magnus Martyr hold
> Inexplicable splendour of Ionian white and gold.

(ll.257–265)

The effect of the music upon Ferdinand was to reduce the anguish of his personal grief, to induce a profound state of receptivity and to lead him to Miranda with whom he is to fall in love. In *The Waste Land*, the music, permeating the streets that lead towards the heart of London, enables the Narrator to address the City in a tone radically different from that of 'The Burial of the Dead'. In a mood of sorrow and appeal rather than one of anger, he creates the experience of one who, straying through its streets, discovers unexpected resources and pleasures. The 'fishmen' of Billingsgate are associated with the fertile life-giving sea and its products. In the middle of the day they relax and are restored, and their masculine virility is linked with the aesthetic, transcendent qualities that Eliot associates with the church of St Magnus Martyr. The seventeenth-century classical decoration of this Wren church in turn suggests the clarity, beauty and heroism of ancient Greece. Here is a powerful antithesis to the 'Unreal City' of the first section of the poem where the faceless commuters, 'undone' by death, flow through streets but a step away from those mentioned here. What has happened? Why, in the middle of a poem of intense and pessimistic criticism of society should there be this oasis o new and positive feelings?

The answer must, at least in part, be related to the emergence of the figure of Tiresias in the episode that intervenes between the two references to *The Tempest* (ll.191–192 and 257). In his note to line 218 Eliot calls him 'the most important personage in the poem, uniting all the rest'. His importance results from his insight, from the depths of his personal suffering and from the complete merging of the Narrator with him. In Greek mythology, Tiresias suffered a number of traumatic experiences: he was transformed for a time into a woman and he was blinded. But he was also given the gifts of long life and prophetic wisdom. Sophocles included him in his great tragedy *Oedipus Rex*, where Tiresias is the blind seer who recognises that the curse that has fallen on Thebes has been caused by Oedipus having unwittingly killed his own father and — again unknowingly — having married his own mother. Here is a prophet who has witnessed a cultural dereliction as profound as that of our own time, a cultural dereliction caused, like that of the Fisher King's 'waste land', by the inability of the king to assume responsibility for his own failure. In *The Waste Land*, Eliot makes Tiresias the personally involved and suffering witness of spiritual impoverishment and so enables the Narrator, now completely one with Tiresias, to move towards his own assumption of personal responsibility.

In the passage from line 215 to line 256, Tiresias is introduced as 'throbbing between two lives'. 'Throbbing' is powerful: it captures the pained intensity of a physically felt awareness, one which combines the 'feminine' capacity for feeling and sympathetic intuition with the 'masculine' capacity for detached thought and analysis. Blind, and yet far-seeing, Tiresias links the sordid, loveless, bedsit sexuality of the typist and her 'small house agent's clerk' with an ancient cursed culture and the Narrator becomes fully committed in his knowledge and experience of 'the dead' of all ages:

> And I Tiresias have foresuffered all
> Enacted on this same divan or bed

> (ll.243–244)

The key words are 'foresuffered' and 'enacted': whilst the young couple enact an artificial charade of assault and submission and are incapable of any feeling, the Narrator is implicated in the fullest emotional sense. Unlike this couple, and unlike all the other characters we have so far encountered in *The Waste Land*, he has confronted death:

> I who have sat by Thebes below the wall
> And walked among the lowest of the dead.

(ll.245–246)

Because his feelings and responses, both of man and of woman, are available to him, he has taken upon himself the suffering of commitment and the pain of alienation that the two actors in this sordid scene so carefully avoid. Now he experiences a glimpse of renewal, for he has known death, the death-in-life of the modern world.

'What the Thunder said' reinforces and develops this transformation of the role of the Narrator: now he stands and walks beside us in our quest for the death that heralds rebirth, he establishes some necessary moral guidelines and, at the last, assumes his responsibility as king in his own 'waste land'. The opening describes that time between the crucifixion of Christ and the coming of the Holy Spirit at Pentecost, a time of uncertainty and of seeking for reassurance. It defines a moment poised on the edge of renewal, when there is knowledge of what is to be done without the conviction of a resurrection:

> We who were living are now dying
> With a little patience

(ll.329–330)

The releasing refreshment of rain is longed for in this time of drought and uncertainty but rain is not to fall within the confines of the poem. Similarly, though the reader is accompanied by the Narrator on the road to Emmaus, the risen Christ remains as yet unrecognised, questionable:

> Who is the third who walks always beside you?

(l.359)

Nevertheless, the assumption throughout is that the resurrected God will bring renewal if the individual can recognise his bankrupt moral state and submit to a greater love. For example, in lines 391–392, we are reminded of Peter who, having denied his connection with Jesus, is forced to recognise — and then weeps for — his faithlessness. This is for him a moment that heralds mighty moral growth and spiritual stature.

Through his threefold interpretation of the utterance of the thunder, Eliot outlines an appropriate attitude for those who await salvation as 'give', 'sympathise', 'control'. Here, indeed, there is still imprisonment —

> . . . each in his prison
> Thinking of the key . . .

(ll.413–414)

— and an emotional release that cannot easily be conveyed to others:

> By this, and this only, we have existed
> Which is not to be found in our obituaries

(ll.405–406)

But Eliot also creates an image that projects the reviving experience of returned affection and of control, exercised not merely for egocentric self-direction (as in the case of those 'who turn the wheel and look to windward' (l.320)), but in the context of loving relationship:

> . . . The boat responded
> Gaily, to the hand expert with sail and oar
> The sea was calm, your heart would have responded
> Gaily, when invited . . .

(ll.418–421)

The repeated and strategically placed 'Gaily' captures a mood new to the poem.

Finally, and most importantly, the Narrator, having acknowledged his brotherhood with man, having become fully identified with Tiresias and the sufferings of the contemporary world and having accompanied us to this anticipation of rebirth, is once again seen:

> I sat upon the shore
> Fishing, with the arid plain behind me
> Shall I at least set my lands in order?

(ll.423–425)

He has moved beyond musing upon the death of father and the wreck of brother: he sees that he must take in hand that which he can control. In accepting his role as Fisher King, he confronts the sea, instead of that limited, land-locked 'dull canal'. There is, it is true, little security in a collapsing environment — 'London Bridge is falling down . . .' and in a fragmentation that includes all values; further growth, further suffering will be required and he may seem mad to other men. But nevertheless, the final, and repeated, word of the poem is 'Shantih', 'the peace which passeth understanding'. And, yes — there is hope in *The Waste Land*.

# AFTERTHOUGHTS

### 1

The 'hope' identified in this essay is largely religious. Can *The Waste Land* be appreciated by an atheist?

### 2

Do you agree with Wilson that the male 'lover' in the first episode of 'A Game of Chess' 'passively suffers the burden of a hysterically demanding woman' (page 86)?

### 3

Compare Wilson's view of Tiresias (pages 89–90) with the views of Pinkney (pages 25–27) and Saunders (page 37–38).

### 4

Is it legitimate to equate any 'voice' within *The Waste Land* with 'that of the poet' (page 83)?

**David Seed**

*David Seed is Lecturer in English at the University of Liverpool, and author of numerous critical articles.*

ESSAY

# Monologue and dialogue in *The Waste Land*

When *The Waste Land* was first published the reviewer Gilbert Seldes spoke for future generations of readers when he wrote that 'it seems at first sight remarkably disconnected' and nowhere is this impression of disconnection stronger that in the abrupt shifts from speaker to speaker. The poem presents a bewildering sequence of voices, some only realized very briefly, which even include the non-human. As we approach the end in section V the sheer noise increases from 'shouting and crying' to the 'song' of the cicada and dry grass, and the voices of the cock crowing and the thunder. The reader is caught uncomfortably between trying to distinguish between all these disparate voices — i.e. to emphasise their differences — and at the same time struggling to relate them to each other. The implication of a method which multiplies speakers is that it is impossible to identify any one voice as Eliot's own. The working title which Eliot used for the poem, 'He do the police in different voices', signals this method very clearly. The line refers to a child mimic in Dickens's *Our Mutual Friend* and transposed to its new context suggests that Eliot was practising a kind of poetical ventriloquism.

In a lecture of 1953 ('The Three Voices of Poetry') Eliot

made clear his view of the relation between an actor and the roles he had to play: 'What we normally hear . . . in the dramatic monologue, is the voice of the poet, who has put on the costume and make-up either of some historical character, or of one out of fiction'[1] It seems to compound our difficulties that Eliot does not usually name his characters, Marie, Madame Sosostris and Tiresias being unusual exceptions. In fact, however, the absence of names means that these figures are not particularised to any great degree and so it becomes proportionately easier for us to read them as characteristic modern cases, representatives of the monotony, inertia and uncertainty, which the poem implies are typical contemporary predicaments. In section III one speaker declares 'I can connect/ Nothing with nothing' (ll.300–301), an unusually overt recognition of a state to which most of the figures in the poem are chronically liable. These words carry important implications for the poem as a whole. The reader's desire to make sense of *The Waste Land* can be related to the anxious search for meaning by some of the characters within the poem. As each new speaker is introduced new possibilities of confusion arise but — even more tantalising — new possibilities of meaning occur.

The economy of the poem is demonstrated in Eliot's hints of character-types and of a whole way of life through brief compressed phrases. Towards the end of section III, for instance, a female speaker outlines an unsatisfactory sexual encounter on the Thames (the main setting of this section is London and London's river) relating her experience to different districts as if she were passively subjected to the actions of the places themselves. 'Highbury bore me. Richmond and Kew/ Undid me' (ll.293–294). The local characteristic of this speaker is a style full of flat direct statements. Hence her section concludes appropriately:

> 'On Margate Sands
> I can connect
> Nothing with nothing
> The broken fingernails of dirty hands.

---

[1] *On Poetry and Poets* (London, 1957), p. 95.

My people humble people who expect
Nothing.'

(ll.300–305)

In the original draft of this part of *The Waste Land* Eliot had
filled out a monologue which left us in no doubt about the social
level of the speaker ('Mine were humble people and conservative/
As neither the rich nor the working class know').[2] The deletions
for the final version of the poem reduce her social identity
to brief suggestions of a middle-class milieu. The speaker is even
less individualised by the resemblances between her experiences
and those of the typist earlier in the section, resemblances
underlined by Eliot's use of rhyming quatrains at each point.
And furthermore she shows a typical characteristic of the
speakers in this poem in that she makes statements without
even drawing out their implications. The flatness of her description is symptomatic and the phrase 'The broken fingernails of
dirty hands' could be read either as a specific encounter or as
an image within the poem's motif of physical squalor.

The experiences or verbal expression of the speakers in *The
Waste Land* are often so minimal that it no longer makes sense
to talk of full 'characters'. Sometimes the speakers appear to
perform only one function. In 'The Burial of the Dead' the
exercise of memory is an activity which links together the
cosmopolitan reminiscences of Marie, the lyrical evocation of the
hyacinth girl, and the man who addresses Stetson. The progression from one to the other takes us farther and farther from
simple description. The first example is simple memory. The
second is a response to the words of the hyacinth girl not placed
within speechmarks because it states the absence of communication ('I could not/ Speak, and my eyes failed . . .'); and yet
one critic has argued that this passage represents the emotional
centre of the poem.[3] The third example (the man who speaks to
Stetson) is the strangest of all since it outrages in turn our sense
of place (London *and* the classical past), of realism (the planted
corpse) and even consistency of language by concluding the

---

[2] *'The Waste Land': A Facsimile and Transcript*, edited by Valerie Eliot (London,
1971), p. 51.
[3] A D Moody, *Thomas Stearns Eliot, Poet* (Cambridge, 1980), p. 81.

section in French. The reader's bearings at such points are strongly influenced by which particular pronouns are in use; 'we', for instance, drawing us dramatically into the experiences of the speakers. Or again Eliot will exploit particular kinds of conversational address which also draw the reader into a dramatic situation. The use of the phrase 'thank you' in line 57, for instance, temporarily puts the reader in the position of a customer receiving (and paying for) information from a 'famous clairvoyante'. The last lines of section I disconcertingly evoke another dramatic situation but then use colloquial language to introduce the sort of symbolic details (of planting and growth) which we would not expect in speech. Here we may be witnessing a foretaste of the combination of poetry and drama which Eliot was to practise in such plays as *The Family Reunion*.

With Madame Sosostris we encounter not only a new voice in section I, but new structural factors. As a spiritual fraud she seems to have been based partly on two characters from Aldous Huxley's first novel, *Crome Yellow* (1921), which satirises a weekend gathering at a country house. In this novel one woman spends her time drawing up horoscopes and another (male) member of the group dresses up for the village fair as 'Sesostris, the Sorceress of Ecbatana.'[4] Eliot composes a pointedly ironic portrait which brings out the self-importance of the fortune-teller and which deflates her pretentions by playing on the visionary and prosaic meanings of 'see' (seeing is in fact one of the major themes of the poem). Madame Sosostris in other words joins the sequence of socially identifiable types which populate the poem. By drawing cards she performs another role which is suggested by Eliot's note to line 46. The figures turned up from the Tarot pack are enumerated here almost like the dramatis personae of a play, and this is an impression which is strengthened by Eliot's explanation of his private associations and of their subsequent appearances in the poem. Leaving aside the specifics of these identifications, Madame Sosostris has a crucial part to play in alerting the reader to the diversity of figures who appear in *The Waste Land.*

---

[4] cf. B C Southam, *A Student's Guide to the Selected Poems of T. S. Eliot* (London, 1977), p. 76.

At this point we need to remember the dramatic nature of the structure of *The Waste Land*. Looking back on his career in 1951 Eliot writes: 'Reviewing my critical output for the last thirty-odd years, I am surprised to find how constantly I have returned to the drama . . .'[5] In fact it isn't a surprise at all since Eliot had been writing plays on an experimental basis since the late 1920s. Before that he had written a series of articles and lectures on Elizabethan and Jacobean dramatists. And earlier still in 1911 he had composed dramatic monologues like 'The Love Song of J. Alfred Prufrock' where the speaker is quite distinct from the author. In a more classic Victorian monologue like Browning's 'My Last Duchess' the duke's unconscious arrogance creates drama by nonchalantly revealing how he disposed of his wife in what amounts to murder, but the sheer dramatic energy of his monologue discourages the reader from criticising him. There is established what the critic Robert Langbaum has called a 'tension between sympathy and moral judgement'.[6] When we move from Browning to Prufrock this tension has largely disappeared because Eliot's monologue is a study in self-consciousness. Prufrock is so agonisingly aware of the figure he cuts in the eyes of others that he composes an ironic externalised image of himself. In spite of his disclaimer ('I am not Prince Hamlet') this is an essentially dramatic strategy. There is no need for the reader to criticise his inertia or the way he evades the present moment because Prufrock is his own harshest critic. His sense of his own absurdity makes Prufrock the first in a whole series of observer-figures who fill Eliot's poems from 'Portrait of a Lady' through to *The Waste Land*. 'Prufrock' is unified by a central consciousness whereas *The Waste Land*, as I have been arguing, assembles together many different consciousnesses. It represents a complication of the monologue tradition rather than a divergence from it. When Madame Sosostris says 'thank you' to her unnamed customer, Eliot implicates the reader temporarily in a search for spiritual substitutes and uses a device of address identical to that employed again and again by Browning to place his speakers in dramatic situ-

---

[5] *Selected Prose of T. S. Eliot*, edited by Frank Kermode (London, 1975), p. 132.
[6] Robert Langbaum, *The Poetry of Experience* (New York, 1963), p. 85.

ations. By virtue of its multiple speakers Robert Langbaum argues that *The Waste Land* uses a *'collage* of voices', linking together written and visual art-forms.[7] The term is well chosen because it suggests mounting different materials on the same canvas, in other words a technique of assembly whereby individual items remain distinct but, because they are juxtaposed in a new and striking way, might add up to an artistic whole. In the collages which the artist Braque composed during the 1910s many of the objects — newspaper cuttings especially — are fragments. In the same way some of Eliot's speakers consist of verbal fragments, resembling snatches of quotation, of overheard conversation or of song. Eliot emphasises the discontinuity between such fragments by suddenly changing verse-form, as in the abrupt shift from song to speech in line 35, or by separating them spatially on the page.

After the first of such gaps in 'The Burial of the Dead' a new kind of voice enters the poem. Drawing on the Old Testament books of Ezekiel and Ecclesiastes, Eliot sets up a speaker with an unusually accusatory relation to the implied listener. Now he questions, forcing the 'you' to find sources of life within the waste land imagery. It would be useful here to contrast Eliot's method with that of the preacher in the book of Ecclesiastes since the latter tries to establish a view that the things of life on earth are 'vain' i.e. empty. He does this by accumulating a series of references to the ending of life through images like the broken cistern or song of the grasshopper which Eliot takes up in his poem. But although Ecclesiastes works in a negative direction there is always a source of hope in the deity: 'Then shall the dust return to the earth as it was: and the spirit shall return unto God who gave it' (12:7). Eliot's speaker begins with a question ('What are the roots that clutch . . .?') and then shifts to direct statements as he points out what is missing in the modern consciousness ('no shelter', 'no relief', 'no sound of water' (ll.23–24). Through these statements he makes it clear that the waste land setting metaphorically reflects the absence of spiritual values, and then offers a gesture of physical relief ('Come in under the shadow of this red rock'). But this gesture

---

[7] Langbaum, p. 77.

turns out to be a prelude to a far more disturbing offer in line 30: 'I will show you fear in a handful of dust.' Eliot plays on the reader's fears without putting forward any hope of the soul reuniting with God. We must remember here that he was not received into the Church of England until 1927. If passages like this one in *The Waste Land* seem to resemble sermons, they are only religious in a negative sense — in pointing out the absence of belief and faith in modern life. In his essay on Matthew Arnold, Eliot declares: 'the essential advantage for a poet is not, to have a beautiful world with which to deal: it is to be able to see beneath both beauty and ugliness; to see the boredom, and the horror, and the glory'.[8] *The Waste Land* consistently evokes the boredom and horror of the contemporary situation but for a suggestion of the 'glory' we have to wait until after Eliot's conversion to Christianity.

It is very risky indeed to privilege any one voice in *The Waste Land*, even that described above. On the verge of his conversion Eliot praised the sermons of Bishop Lancelot Andrewes for representing an authoritative voice but this sort of context is missing in 'The Burial of the Dead', partly because, as usual, the identity of the speaker is in flux.[9] He blurs into the thoughtful fisherman of section III and — even more importantly — into Tiresias. The figure of Tiresias has attracted a lot of critical comment partly because Eliot's note to line 218 makes assertions about the structure of the poem which appeal seductively to the reader's desire to form connections.[10] Tiresias, he tells us, is 'the most important personage in the poem, uniting all the rest', using the term 'personage' in the French sense of a dramatic character. Is this in fact the case? A brief consideration of Tennyson's treatment of the same figure may help to point the way, especially as Eliot knew Tennyson's work well and would almost certainly have been familiar with this particular poem. Tennyson's dramatic monologue 'Tiresias' presents an aged seer yearning for the lost energies and insights of his youth. He is caught in the situational irony of having been

---

[8] *The Use of Poetry and the Use of Criticism* (London, 1964), p. 106.
[9] *Selected Essays* (London, 1951), p. 344.
[10] e.g. Grover Smith, *The Waste Land* (London, 1983), p. 50.

granted access to insights which no one would believe. He is, in short, a diminished and impotent figure. Exactly the same could be said of Eliot's Tiresias who is introduced as a figure of paradox (a man with breasts, he can see but is blind) quite detached from the figures he 'observes' through such clinical verbs as 'perceived', 'enacted' or 'foresuffered'. The urgency of the spiritual voice in section I has attenuated down to the ironic revery of the fisherman and the equally ironic commentary of Tiresias. He points out the typical, predictable nature of the encounter between the typist and the 'young man carbuncular' in a way which distances them from the observer. They become human specimens enacting a meaningless sexual ritual, but Tiresias by the same token becomes a bizarre kind of voyeur, unable to affect their actions in any way. Because of his implied dissociation of feeling from seeing A D Moody has argued that Tiresias represents the 'dead heart' of *The Waste Land*.[11] Although in his note Eliot describes Tiresias as a 'mere spectator' this role is potentially very important. In 1917 Eliot published a short story called 'Eeldrop and Appleplex', revolving around two observers of urban life. Eeldrop excitedly describes a rare experience where a Spaniard they have met briefly stops being a type and takes on a unique individuality — but this is an exception to the general run of events. He complains: 'The majority not only have no language to express anything save generalized man; they are for the most part unaware of themselves as anything but generalized men'.[12] The awareness of characters in *The Waste Land* either matches this account or is even more atrophied, and Eeldrop's indignation at seeing people as types is compounded by the notion of a 'detached observer'. Tiresias is exactly such a figure whose perspective diminishes the humanity of those he observes. His ineffectuality confirms that he too is subject to the common malaise of the whole problem.

The encounter between the typist and the clerk is astonishing because it is silent. The stress in these lines is entirely on what can be seen so that, although Tiresias addresses the

---

[11] Moody, p. 92.
[12] 'Eeldrop and Appleplex', *Little Review* 4 (1917), p. 10.

reader, his relation to the other two characters is essentially a visual one. This is the point where we need to consider dialogue and its function within *The Waste Land* and here an earlier poem can be helpful. 'Portrait of a Lady' describes what should be a social meeting, a situation where dialogue should take place. The older lady has composed the scene almost with a sense of theatre, to set up a context for what is essentially a monologue where she casts the young man as a foil to her own histrionic suffering. Ironically she claims intimate communication when none is taking place: 'How much it means that I say this to you'. While she is speaking aloud her visitor is silently reflecting on the absurdity of the whole situation and the disparity between the two voices in this poem undermines the very possibility of dialogue. The expectations of the situation have not been realised. *The Waste Land*, too, is a poem about absences. The empty chapel ('only the wind's home') in section V is typical of the poem as a whole in being the location of an activity which is no longer taking place. Again and again Eliot raises expectations of religious observance and romantic meeting which never materialise. Spiritual faith and love are signalled as gaps, the latter emerging clearly in 'A Game of Chess'.

The meeting at the beginning of this section resembles the situation in 'Portrait of a Lady'. A setting is described, this time in cloying lush detail before the woman enters. Once she starts to speak, however, differences emerge:

> 'My nerves are bad to-night. Yes, bad. Stay with me.
> 'Speak to me. Why do you never speak? Speak.
>    'What are you thinking of? What thinking? What?
> 'I never know what you are thinking. Think.'
>
> I think we are in rats' alley
> Where the dead men lost their bones.
>
> 'What is that noise?'
>                        The wind under the door.
> 'What is that noise now?   What is the wind doing?'
>                        Nothing again nothing.

(ll.111–120)

Eliot has taken the first lines more or less directly from D H

Lawrence's novella *The Fox* where exchanges take place between two women (Banford and March) clearly contrasted as opposite emotional types, the former being nervous the latter calmer and more thoughtful.[13] Eliot has cut out the answers to create another psuedo-dialogue where the silent 'answers' of the listener reveal the meaninglessness of the occasion. But whereas the speaker in 'Portrait of a Lady' was insulated by her own theatricality, this speaker is far more urgent, demonstrating a panicked awareness of the other's indifference. Eliot brilliantly captures this quality through the progression in the first four lines from statements or questions to desperate imperatives. The very arrangement of the lines on the page suggests the gap between the two figures, questions being balanced against replies which are not replies since they are out of speech marks. The difference between this passage and 'Portrait of a Lady' is that more is at stake. It is typical of *The Waste Land* that questions are not met with any meaningful responses so that we are left with indications of the *desire* for dialogue rather than its realisation.

It is particularly ironic that Eliot should use such colloquial English to convey the absence of communication and it is important to remember that he had strong reservations about a certain kind of dramatic poetry. In a dialogue-essay of 1928 he wrote: 'At the present time there is a manifest preference for the "conversational" in poetry — the style of "direct speech", opposed to the "oratorical" and the rhetorical.' Eliot disliked this crude opposition, arguing that rhetoric had a much broader range of utterance than this fashion would imply. He continues that the finest rhetoric in Shakespeare 'occurs in situations where a character in the play *sees himself* in a dramatic light' and cites as one example Enobarbus's view of Cleopatra in the lines beginning 'the barge she sat in'.[14] This is exactly the passage to which Eliot alludes in the opening of 'A Game of Chess', where both the grand figure under observation and the observer are smothered by an over-detailed setting and diminished further by the non-exchange described above. Eliot's

---

[13] cf. Southam, p. 80.
[14] *Selected Essays*, pp. 38, 39.

comments on the conversational take us directly into the most colloquial section of the poem, the pub scene which concludes 'A Game of Chess'. Here a former dialogue is retold as a monologue, one incidentally which Eliot made a point of reading with a strong Cockney accent. The monotonous tag-phrases 'I said', 'she said' highlight the social level of the speaker who is obscurely threatening Lil. Lil herself is established as the victim of a socially typical predicament (a loveless marriage) which the speaker is trying to draw to her awareness. Once again distances are created with the dialogue (is the speaker disinterested or has she got her eye on Lil's husband?) and between the speaker and reader. The emphasised social register of the language once again classes the speaker as a type-figure to be looked at. Indeed if we were drawn sympathetically into her narrative this interest would not be fulfilled because characteristically the section tails off inconclusively.

In the encounter between the typist and the clerk physical action seems to act like a substitute for dialogue. Again and again in *The Waste Land* Eliot implies that the absence of verbal communication reflects a lack of emotional contact. Love is referred to constantly but always as something missing or degraded. Near the beginning of section II Eliot introduces a reference to the story of Philomel who was raped by her brother-in-law, Tereus king of Thrace (named in line 206). She is transformed into a nightingale who 'Filled all the desert with inviolable voice' (l.101). 'Inviolable' is a very important term here because it sets up a contrast between the purity of Philomel's voice and the sterile landscape; and even more importantly makes a contrast with the 'dirty ears' (l.103) which hear her song. Eliot takes up this same story in section III where love-songs are degraded by being associated with the sordid sexual encounters and equally sordid environment of contemporary London. As usual in the poem the lyrical voice of Philomel indicates not contact but rather distance — the distance between romantic ideals and the nature of modern life.

In section V, however, Eliot appears to have devised a new voice which now articulates a *common* awareness of absence and loss instead of assembling individual instances. The 'we' which orchestrates the waste land imagery seems much more inclusive than any previous usage and as such alleviates the gloom of the poem which grows out of isolation and the distances between figures. Now reader and speaker temporarily come together in a marginally increased awareness of a common predicament of spiritual loss. The speaker at this point addresses a companion as they walk across an arid landscape which marks a significant advance out of the individual inertia of earlier speakers. Without an ultimate goal ever quite materialising — we have to wait until *Four Quartets* for that — walking sets up the new speaker's articulation of desire ('If there were water . . ') and his interrogation of impressions ('Who is the third who walks always beside you?', 'What is that sound high in the air?') without ever claiming privileges of special insight. There are in fact reasons against concluding that this section of the poem has become more affirmative. Firstly the positive spiritual implications of some lines are offset by the suggestion of madness and hallucination in the vision of inverted towers or the image taken from *Dracula* of 'bats with baby faces' crawling 'head downward down a blackened wall' (ll.379–385). Secondly, the inclusive voice splits apart back into the individual first person (lines 410, 423, 430). And finally the voice of the thunder is ambiguous. Although Eliot distinguishes typographically between the latter — three Sanskrit terms (which would be incomprehensible without his note) — and the surrounding lines, the capital letters suggest volume and make the repeated 'DA' stand out on the page (but without necessarily indicating meaning). The capitalised refrain in the pub scene could similarly be taken either as the voice of a publican or as an external voice trying to inject an urgency into the situation. The thunder is even more ambiguous because it could be giving an apocalyptic warning of impending doom or it could be meaningless noise; the title 'What the Thunder said' draws on the biblical presentation of thunder as a voice of God to make us expect a message but never actually satisfies our desire for meaning. One repeated question hangs over Eliot's use of different speakers in *The Waste Land*: will they ever come together? The collective voice which opens section V seems to suggest that they have, but the proliferation of sounds suggests the very opposite. In the last lines the poem breaks down into a babble of different languages — Italian, Latin, French, and Sanskrit. The fragmentation of voices persists to the very end of *The Waste Land*.

# AFTERTHOUGHTS

## 1

What arguments are put forward in this essay to justify Eliot's 'poetical ventriloquism' (page 94)?

## 2

Do you agree that 'seeing . . . is one of the major themes of the poem' (page 97)?

## 3

Do you agree that there is no suggestion of 'glory' in *The Waste Land* (page 100)?

## 4

Would *The Waste Land* make a good play?

**Andrew Gibson**

*Andrew Gibson is Lecturer in English Literature at Royal Holloway and Bedford New College, University of London.*

ESSAY

# Sexuality in *The Waste Land*

One of the central concerns in Eliot's work is the clash between the claims of the world and those of the spirit. His poetry repeatedly suggests a desire to escape or 'transcend' ordinary reality. But reality exerts a firm hold. 'Transcendence' may be difficult if not impossible to achieve. Right from the start, Eliot's poetry presents the real world as basically unappealing. But reality also has its traps and temptations. Eliot and the characters in his poetry often have no certain faith in spiritual things. That makes the world's temptations all the harder to resist. The real world is a source of chronic dissatisfaction and despair. But when there are no spiritual securities, it may seem the only possible source of any kind of comfort.

Sexuality obviously has a very important place in Eliot's poetry. For Eliot sees sexuality as what is most at odds with spirituality. The poems tend to present it as an important potential 'distraction', but also a principal cause of dismay. In general, during the course of his career, Eliot's poetry moves increasingly towards religious faith, and away from any attachment to the world. But *The Waste Land* is very much a point of transition in this development. In 'The Love Song of J. Alfred Prufrock' (1910–11), Prufrock is ironically resigned to reality.

There seems to be nothing else for it. On the other hand, 'Ash Wednesday' (1927–30) is written after Eliot joined the Church of England and is a poem about spiritual striving. *The Waste Land* was largely written in 1921 and 1922. It comes halfway between 'Prufrock' and 'Ash Wednesday', and seems suspended between the two different kinds of attitude to be found in them. As we might expect, then, Eliot's treatment of the theme of sexuality in *The Waste Land* is particularly complex and, in some ways, rather uncertain.

The most obvious aspect of Eliot's handling of the theme is his distaste for modern sexuality — the kinds of sexuality evident in the society the poem describes. Eliot makes the point most clearly in the second and third parts of the poem, 'A Game of Chess' and 'The Fire Sermon'. The main subject in both is sexuality and sexual relationships. 'The Fire Sermon' gets its title from a sermon of the Buddha's, as Eliot tells us in his Notes to the poem. The Buddha preached the fire sermon against all the human passions, and not just sexual passion, though sexual passion was included. But the main concern of the fire sermon in *The Waste Land* is sex. Eliot effectively gives an ironical equivalent of the Buddha's sermon. His point is that the world of *The Waste Land* is *not* 'on fire', as the Buddha's fire sermon tells us his world is, with 'the fire of passion . . . the fire of hatred, with the fire of infatuation'. It's a dismally passionless world. The sexual encounters the third section of the poem refers us to seem fleeting or devitalised.

In Eliot's *Waste Land*, sexuality is an essentially diminished thing. In the case of the couple in 'A Game of Chess', for instance, we get little more than a sense of sheer human poverty and emptiness, 'Nothing again nothing' (l.120). Lil's world (ll.139–172) is a brutal one, a world of crude sexual competition. 'Others can pick and choose if you can't,' her friend warns her (l.154). Abortions and premature ageing are among the likely consequences of Lil's kind of life. In 'The Fire Sermon', again, the 'nymphs' have apparently been deserted by 'their friends, the loitering heirs of city directors' (ll.179–180). Certainly, the latter 'have left no addresses' (l.181). The clerk and the typist's brief piece of sexual 'folly' is a matter of boredom, fatigue, 'vanity' and 'indifference' (ll.241–242). The girl who is 'undone' by 'Richmond and Kew' adopts an oddly formal tone for her sexual encounter ('After the event ... I made no comment', ll.297–299), which effectively crushes any hint of feeling. She can't even understand why she might want to 'resent' the man in question. In 'The Fire Sermon' at least, coldly exploiting women seems to be the most common form of sexual activity in the *Waste Land*. Eliot repeats the word 'departed', and the repetition emphasises the transient quality of the liaisons. He also repeats the word 'wept', and that should make us aware that, in the middle part of the poem, there are other feelings in play apart from disgust. At the beginning of 'The Fire Sermon', for instance, the speaker sits down and weeps after calling the nymphs and their friends to mind (l.182). Similarly, the speaker at the end of 'A Game of Chess' bids a sad farewell to the 'ladies' in the words uttered by Shakespeare's Ophelia shortly before she drowns herself (l.172). In both cases, there is a tone of despair that is actually stronger than the sense of distaste. Indeed, there is more than a little despair, in the middle part of the poem, at what Eliot takes to be the squalor of contemporary sexuality.

The sense of present squalor is enhanced by the contrasts that Eliot develops between it and images of sexuality drawn from history and the mythology, literature and culture of the past. Eliot saw James Joyce's novel, *Ulysses*, as 'manipulating a continuous parallel between contemporaneity and antiquity', comparing and contrasting past and present. He attempted to do the same himself in *The Waste Land*, and it affects his presentation of sexual themes. The futility of the couple's relationship in 'A Game of Chess', stands out more clearly in contrast to some of the literature referred to in the opening passage (ll.77–103). Line 77, for instance, echoes lines from Shakespeare's *Antony and Cleopatra* (II.2.190). In Shakespeare's play, a character called Enobarbus is paying tribute to Cleopatra's beauty, and describing her first meeting with her lover, Antony. Enobarbus then goes on to tell us, that 'age cannot wither' Cleopatra, 'nor custom stale her infinite variety'. But Cleopatra's kind of splendour, her 'infinite variety' is precisely what Eliot's vacuous, neurotic woman lacks. Here, Eliot means us to recall a little of Shakespeare's scene, so we can grasp the point more firmly. The grandeur and intensity of Shakespeare's two lovers shed a critical light on Eliot's own hollow couple, and their depleted vitality. Other references work in similar ways — references to Sappho, Chaucer, Spenser, Marvell, Actaeon and Diana, Elizabeth I and the Earl of Leicester. Eliot repeatedly 'manipulates' the past and its culture to a point where it passes judgement on the modern world. In all the cases I've mentioned, it passes a harsh judgement on the shallowness, for Eliot, of modern sexuality.

But Eliot's treatment of the relationship between past and present in *The Waste Land* is more complicated than this, and so is its relevance to the sexual theme. For one thing, the poem's references to the past and its literature aren't always set in contrast to the present. The present sometimes seems to mirror the past. Certain references to the past only reflect, enhance and deepen our sense of the insufficiency and emptiness of the present. The poem suggests, for instance, that longing and loneliness are dominant features of (comparatively futile) present-day experience. But some of the literary allusions in the poem are themselves allusions to images of longing and loneliness. For example, early in 'The Burial of the Dead', a voice tells us of 'the hyacinth girl', and of his own eyes failing. Eliot follows the passage with the words '*Oed' und leer das Meer*' ('Waste and empty the sea', l.42). They come from Wagner's opera *Tristan und Isolde*, and they're sung by Tristan himself, as he lies dying, waiting for his lover Isolde to arrive from across the sea. Here, the sense of bleakness and deprivation in the opera actually matches up with the sense of bleakness and deprivation in Eliot's poem. In *The Waste Land*, part of Eliot seems to be making a point about the superiority of attitudes to sexuality in the past. But part of him isn't convinced of the point. The allusion, for instance, in the title 'A Game of Chess' is to a play by the Jacobean dramatist, Thomas Middleton, called *Women Beware Women*. But in fact *Women Beware Women* is itself a play which sees sexuality in very dark terms, and Eliot's actual reference is to a scene in which one character distracts another's attention while the powerful duke forces the young, married Bianca to have sex with him. Eliot means us to call the scene to mind. His Notes to his poem explicitly point us to it.

Here, as elsewhere in the poem, an image of sexuality from the past proves to be as disquieting as those Eliot gives us from the present. Eliot knows, too, that the past was also quite as

capable of trivialising sex as the present. The 'inviolable v
of the nightingale in 'A Game of Chess', for instance, is merely
'Jug Jug' to dirty ears (ll.100–103). Eliot seems to be saying
something, here, about the way in which vulgar minds take the
romance out of sex. (The allusion is partly to the romantic poet
Keats, and his 'Ode to a Nightingale'.) But the vulgar minds in
question aren't modern, they are Elizabethan. It was the Eliz-
abethans who used 'jug jug' as a crude phrase for having sex.
Similarly, the poem tells us that violation, cold seduction and
callous exploitation are all aspects of 'waste land sexuality'. But
the most extreme and brutal image of that kind in the poem is
an ancient one: the image of Philomela, raped by Tereus, who
also cut out her tongue (ll.99–100). It's an important image in
the poem. Eliot actually comes back to it, giving us Philomela's
pained, despairing cry when we're some way into 'The Fire
Sermon' (l.206).

So *The Waste Land* is not just negative about modern
sexuality. It often seems negative about sexuality in general,
sexuality as part of human being. Indeed, the very first lines of
the poem seem to express a conviction of the futility of any 'stirring' of 'dull roots', of 'breeding', of the continual returns of
spring, and its vital renewals (ll.1–4). In 'A Game of Chess',
Eliot reminds us that the world still 'pursues' its sexual
pleasures, in spite of the ever-present facts of pain and disappointment (l.102). But his tone is weary here. The last section
of 'A Game of Chess' conveys a similar sense of the urgent
pressure and (for Eliot) the weary, inevitable sameness of the
pursuit. But, above all, it is Tiresias in 'The Fire Sermon' who
generalises and universalises the sense of sexual disillusion so
often present in the poem. Tiresias tells us, for example, that
he 'perceived the scene' involving the clerk and the typist and
then 'foretold the rest' (l.229). He informs us that he (or she) has
'foresuffered all/ Enacted on this same divan or bed' (ll.243–444).
At these moments, he seems to be presenting the scene as
possibly a type of all sexual encounters, and not just modern
ones. He implies that this is the way the (disparagingly named)
'human engine' commonly works (l.216). The classical Tiresias
was associated with wisdom and prophecy, and the association
enhances the effect here. So, too, does the fact that Tiresias was
both male and female, as here (an 'Old man with wrinkled

female breasts', 1.219). Eliot makes Tiresias seem to speak for both sexes, with a knowledge that is relevant to both. We should also remember that, in his Notes to *The Waste Land*, Eliot said that Tiresias was 'the most important personage in the poem, uniting all the rest'. For Eliot, what 'Tiresias sees' is 'the substance of the poem'. In other words, an image of empty, futile sex is at the very heart of *The Waste Land*.

At this point the poem may seem to fall into place. If it's negative about sexuality in general, then we can begin to understand its structure. 'The Burial of the Dead' sets the scene. In 'A Game of Chess' and 'The Fire Sermon', Eliot takes us through a variety of disillusioned rejections of the human world, which hinge on a set of negative responses to human sexuality. Then the brief fourth section of the poem tells us not to trust in worldly things. The world of those concerned with 'profit and loss' is a matter of indifference to Phlebas now. So, too, is the world of practical hope and struggle and endeavour, of 'you who turn the wheel and look to windward' (1.320). The world attaches a false value and importance to beauty, too. If Phlebas 'was once handsome and tall' (1.321), we are asked to 'consider' what has become of him. 'What the Thunder said' then begins a tentative exploration of spiritual possibilities. Eliot will explore them further in 'Ash Wednesday'. This is a reading of the poem that leaves Tiresias very firmly at its centre. A general distaste for human sexuality plays a central role in the poem's movement away from the things of this world to spiritual matters. The poem expresses its distaste for sexuality most fully through Tiresias.

Part of Eliot clearly thought that there was a kind of 'centre' or 'essence' to the poem. He identified it with Tiresias. But the poet of *The Waste Land* was also thinking, feeling and writing in discontinuous and fragmented ways. Because of that, it's hard to see the poem as really having any 'centre', and our description of its structure is therefore only part of the story. This lack of 'centre' is particularly evident in Eliot's treatment of sexuality in the poem. The sense of sex as generally empty, futile and trivial is present in the poem, but by no means always present. Eliot is capable of conveying other attitudes to sexuality, too. As we've seen already, he calls to mind some very different images of sexuality as they are provided, for instance, by the literature of the past. Even in *The Waste Land* itself, at moments, he associates sexuality with a fierce intensity that is quite unlike the typist's boredom and fatigue. This is the case with the pained but powerful voice that abruptly takes over at the end of 'The Fire Sermon':

> To Carthage then I came
>
> Burning burning burning burning
> O Lord Thou pluckest me out
> O Lord Thou pluckest
>
> burning

(ll.307–311)

I suggested earlier that the relation between Eliot's 'fire sermon' and the Buddha's was largely ironic. But here, at the very end of 'The Fire Sermon', we suddenly hear a different kind of voice. Most of the other figures in 'The Fire Sermon' have appeared to be simply incapable of the Buddha's 'fire of passion'. But this is a speaker who really is tormented by it. He seems to be struggling (in vain) to sustain his faith in a God who will deliver him from a world of 'burning' passions. In the end, he resigns himself to the 'fire'. Here, Eliot is clearly thinking primarily of sexual passion. That's clear from the references to St Augustine's *Confessions*. They allude to the temptation of 'unholy loves' which Augustine vainly sought to resist in his youth.

It's hard to reconcile this fierily tormented personage at the end of 'The Fire Sermon' with the indifference or disgust elsewhere in Eliot's poem. Other figures give us a sense of the world as sexual waste land. The Augustine-like voice gives us the impression that it's a sexual inferno. This points us to something important in *The Waste Land*. The dominant attitudes to sexuality in it are negative ones. But there's variety to the negativity, and even some degree of uncertainty as to the most appropriate *kind* of negativity. Furthermore, the poem sometimes appears to question or modify its presentation of sexuality as a whole. At moments at least, it allows for alternatives — partly because, as we've already seen, it isn't really a poem with a 'centre', or with the kind of certainty that having a 'centre' would produce. Thus Eliot can occasionally even warm to the sexuality of his creatures, if only in an indirect way: Marie's, for example (ll.15–16), and even Albert and Lil's (ll.166–167). Unexpectedly, sexuality can even turn out to be a positive. Towards the end of the poem, for instance, one of the voices hints at the virtue of 'surrender':

> My friend, blood shaking my heart
> The awful daring of a moment's surrender
> Which an age of prudence can never retract
> By this, and this only, we have existed

(ll.402–405)

This doesn't necessarily refer to sexual 'surrender' of course. But it's about a full, intense, passionate and whole surrender — to God, perhaps, but possibly also to another human being. It might include the sexual, as the phrase about 'blood' shaking the 'heart' might suggest. The idea is certainly expressed in partly sexual terms.

When it's a question of 'antiquity', of course, or references to 'antiquity', as we've already seen, sexuality is more likely to emerge as a clear positive. To take another example of this, when he wrote *The Waste Land*, Eliot used a book by Jessie Weston called *From Ritual to Romance*. He was particularly interested in her account of a figure who appeared in old myths called the Fisher King. According to Jessie Weston, in a number of old myths the Fisher King appeared as an impotent figure, whose land was infertile. Both needed regeneration. This implied the positive, health-giving, fertilising nature of vital forces, including sexual ones. The various references to the Fisher King in *The Waste Land* carry this implication. So do other references to figures in a similar state of anticipation, or similarly awaiting some sort of return or fulfilment. Thus, for instance, with the reference to the sailor in Wagner's opera *Tristan und Isolde* thinking of his '*Irisch Kind*' (his Irish girl (l.33)); or the reference to the spirit Ariel leading Prince Ferdinand to the beautiful Miranda in Shakespeare's *The Tempest* (l.48). Eliot's poem partly suggests that the present world is a sexual waste land because sex itself is empty and futile. But, contradictorily, it also suggests that the present world is a waste land because it lacks the ancient world's vital sense of sexuality as an elemental force.

Unlike Eliot's other poems, *The Waste Land* cannot be

thought of as spoken by a single voice, or by the poet's own voice. It's a tissue of different voices. They blend and mingle with each other, and so do the different perspectives they introduce. We can identify a range of different speakers in *The Waste Land*, and that's partly what makes it seem more of a panorama, more of a statement about a society or a culture than Eliot's other poems. It also reflects the fact that in some ways *The Waste Land* is a more complex and uncertain work than they are. There are conflicts in attitude in *The Waste Land*, not least, as we've seen, in its treatment of the theme of sexuality. This fits in with its essentially tentative nature. The Eliot of *The Waste Land* isn't fond of the world, of course, and can't affirm its pleasures. But he is not so convinced of religious alternatives that he can afford categorically to reject the world. *The Waste Land* is partly an exploratory poem, and it's also a poem of moods, without a single, clear, consistent direction or purpose. It circles around the theme of sexuality, as it circles around the themes of religion and death. It develops a certain consistency of response to them, but without forcing that consistency into a set of fixed conclusions. It suggests that certain attitudes may be of central relevance to sexual experience, but also makes us doubt how 'central' they can really be.

# AFTERTHOUGHTS

## 1

What do you understand by 'Transcendence' (opening paragraph)?

## 2

What similarities and differences does Gibson identify between Elizabethan and twentieth-century sexuality?

## 3

'The poem expresses its distaste for sexuality most fully through Tiresias' (page 112). Do you agree?

## 4

What do you understand by Gibson's claim that *The Waste Land* isn't really a poem with a 'centre' (page 113)?

**John Cunningham**

*John Cunningham was until recently Head of English at Varndean Sixth Form College. He is the author of numerous critical studies.*

## ESSAY

# Does the reader need a guide to *The Waste Land?*

This extraordinary poem has been seen as the classic statement of post-war disillusion; as a private expression of personal depression; even as a kind of learned joke, complete with an apparatus of Notes which makes it appear less, not more, accessible. Eliot himself professed to be surprised at the first interpretation; the second seems inadequate in that most serious poems could be said to have been written at least partly because the writer had something in his system which he wanted to get out of it; the third seems even less likely when it is known that the Notes were written only to add bulk to a poem of a length not convenient to publish on its own.

We also know, because he was to say more about it after he became famous, something of Eliot's own problem in writing it. All poets writing in English up to his time had known that their educated readers had been educated in the same way — with a classical bias — so they could all call upon the same set of references and be sure they would be understood. In our century, however, different people may be very highly educated in quite different ways, and what used to be the universal pattern is today probably the rarest: very few people now have a classical background. How then is a poet to write for such a disparate audience? Eliot himself, with a cosmopolitan education from both America and Europe, coined a phrase for his own goal — the 'objective correlative', that is an image to which everyone could respond. But someone coming for the first time to *The Waste Land* might well feel that there was nothing whatever which created any response at all. By examining three ways of approaching this work — those of the academic, the idealist and the student with an eye to examinations — we may arrive at a method for ourselves.

A scholar probably comes to this poem seeking to enhance his academic reputation, and would call this essay 'The Centrality of the Esoteric in Early Middle Eliot' or something equally off-putting. His work is addressed to other scholars and may help ordinary readers precious little, though it is worth noticing that Eliot, like James Joyce (whose *Ulysses* was published in Paris in the same year that *The Waste Land* was brought out in America, 1922) has indeed provided a fruitful ground for deep, academic analysis.

At the other extreme stands the idealist: the reader who believes that a poem should be experienced, not studied. He will read the poem aloud — if he can manage the large number of different languages involved — or listen to a good recording of it. Such a reader cannot help those of us who feel the need to 'understand' the poem, but his method is a good one. The poem reads extremely well, for Eliot had an excellent ear, and we can learn a lot about it by listening. If anyone doubts this, we may try it out by plunging into the middle and reading the last part of 'A Game of Chess' in good, twanging Cockney:

> You ought to be ashamed, I said, to look so antique.
> (And her only thirty-one.)

(ll.156–157)

It is remarkable that this was written by a thirty-four-year-old American.

*Listening* to the poem, then, may be more rewarding than we might think — and that should be true of any good poem. Yet many of us still come to this particular work because we have to or we think we ought to: it is 'significant'. It is on a syllabus. It will be 'examined'. We have to try to understand it. It is worth examining in detail what an anxious student — as opposed to the academic and the idealist we have mentioned — might find himself faced with merely in getting from the title-page to the first line, and to see how much he can achieve — or lose — by laboriously following every reference to its source, and beyond, for the source alone is not enough for those who annotate. That, indeed, is the problem of allusions, a key word in the study of Eliot, and the title-page is a mass of them.

Most of us will recognise that there are four languages on the page, of which we may well understand only the English. A translation does not seem to help a great deal: 'For I have seen the Cumaean Sybil with my own eyes hanging in a jar and the boys that were there with her said "Sybil, what do you want?" She replied "I want to die".' 'For Ezra Pound, the better maker.' The Latin and Greek is from Petronius Arbiter, the Italian from Dante. Of Ezra Pound we may know nothing, or that he was a Fascist sympathiser, or that he wrote poems which look even more fragmentary than this one, which is not helpful. Further research brings the information that Pound did help Eliot (and us, we may think) by going through the first version of this poem and cutting it severely, so proving himself the better maker, or poet — for which 'maker' is the word that Chaucer would have used. Why bring in Dante to say so? Because the passage quoted is one that Eliot found exceptionally moving. In his vision of Purgatory, Dante imagines meeting a poet he greatly admired, Arnaut Daniel, and pays him the greatest compliment that one writer can offer to another: he writes a short passage in the language — Provençal — of the earlier, 'better' maker of verses.

This seems a very private allusion indeed. Petronius Arbiter, on the other hand, is public property nowadays, though he was not when the poem was written, for his *Satyricon* was one of the most famous indecent books of the Western world and was hard to obtain except in the original racy Latin. The central comic character, Trimalchio, is a gross fellow who was a slave and has now become free and exceedingly rich. He shows off his wealth in the most vulgar fashion, and the two heroes of the story attend a lavish and sickening feast he gives. He shows off not only his wealth but his knowledge of the world: when the ancient woman, the Sybil of Cumae who had the gift of prophecy, is mentioned, she is dismissed in the passage quoted. A little

Greek will tell us that the boys were disrespectful too, for they address her in the singular, which would be quite improper.

Long before we get to Greek singulars we might be asking what a bizarre work of AD 60 has to do with 1922. Yet we already have an answer. The gross Trimalchio, full of his own importance, knowing the price of everything and the value of nothing, is with us yet: he is the self-made man who worships his maker. A particularly unpleasant form of this man had emerged in the Great War, when huge profits were to be made out of the exploitation of suffering. If we look in the pages of the satirical English journal *Punch* just after the end of that war we shall see the modern Trimalchio in the flash dress of the Wartime Profiteer. A war that cost ten million lives and did incalculable harm leaves behind it nothing but this gross, successful survivor — is that the point of the allusion? And that the wisdom learnt by age is that all life becomes a burden?

Having arrived at this assumption we may feel that we do, at all events, have some understanding of the title-page, so we may start on the poem.

The first line — 'April is the cruellest month' — is famous, but why is it famous? Is it because it is unexpected? Spring is a season about which traditional poets burble happily but not always convincingly: perhaps Eliot simply means to surprise us into seeing that this poem is going to be different. Is it, on the other hand, because it is true? A time of hope, of rebirth, may make us very conscious of how little hope we have or how little of our potential we ever bring to birth. Is it a private reference? Eliot was suffering from severe depression at the time he wrote it and it is now known that depressives feel worst in the spring — April has the highest suicide rate of any month. Is it a very scholarly allusion? Eliot was interested in the origins of religion, in the fertility myths and rituals which may be the basis of all man's attempts to find a mystic meaning in his world, so this might refer to that most anxious time of the year when our ancestors prayed — literally for their lives — that the winter was indeed gone and that the new season might bring plenty, not want.

The anxious student we have supposed to be studying the poem may by now feel that he is suffering from plenty and to spare: he has so far read one line of the poem and found many ways of reading it. Tiring, perhaps, he peeps at the end. In the last paragraph of the poem (ll.433–423) he sees some five languages, Modern and Elizabethan English amongst them; quotations from obscure Latin and a popular nursery rhyme; a line from a French poem (which had a Spanish title) by Gerard de Nerval, a man who used to lead a lobster about on a ribbon. He may begin to wish he had opted for another set book and to suspect that he will never finish with this one.

No one does finish with it. The poem has the ability to be read and re-read over many years (I can testify to forty) and still present new facets and insights. What we need is an approach somewhere between the extremes of the person who says we have only to listen to it and the worried note-taker whose anxieties we have been following. What does the average reader, if he exists, need to know to get at the poem?

We shall not get at it at all if we succumb to fashionable jargon and thought, and dismiss Eliot as an 'élitist' poet. Eliot read widely and did not see why he should not draw on his reading to expand his writing. Like most of us he was human enough to be coy about his own ignorance, and the best note that he wrote (on line 46), which runs 'I am not familiar with the exact constitution of the Tarot pack', will be gleefully seized upon as an admission that he had never seen one. Now available in any good bookshop, Tarot cards were not easily come by in 1922, but if he had never owned them, presumably we do not need to know much about them either. Most of us know, as he did, that they contain a series of single cards with symbols, and when Eliot names them the names are largely self-explanatory. So Madame Sosostris, her ambiguous fortune-telling further blurred by catarrh (l.45) deals out the Wheel (of Fortune) the Hanged Man (the Crucifixion) and a 'blank . . ./ Which I am forbidden to see' (l.54–55) which is surely the Future. She knows no more of it than anyone else but is making money out of anxiety. When traditional gods seem to have failed us, as in terrible wars, we turn to the mystic fringe and this phoney, with her false 'Egyptian' name and her genteel 'Thank you' as the essential fee is paid, has become 'known to be the wisest woman in Europe' (l.45). In examining this brief episode we have come upon an important truth: the more we know about the things that Eliot knew, the deeper our understanding may become, if we are not smothered by detail — but a *little* knowledge intelligently applied can take us a good way into the poem.

A little knowledge of what? Looking through the section in which the clairvoyante appears we can see the opening fifteen lines or so assume a little understanding of the international aristocratic society of Europe which was destroyed by the events of 1914. They were interrelated — 'My cousin . . . the arch-duke' — they spoke very colloquial German with ease, they could escape the harshness of the world whenever they wanted to. The survivor, Marie, says 'I read, much of the night, and go south in the winter' (l.18), which is in the present tense. Now her escape is to pass a sleepless night lost in a book, to avoid the dark season by travelling to a sunnier place. Some understanding of the huge change in Europe that the Great War accelerated or created is surely as necessary as it is reasonable.

In the middle passage of this section ('What are the roots that clutch . . .', l.19) some modest biblical awareness might help, if it extends only to the fairly common knowledge that in the Bible shade, green pastures, above all water, are signs of peace or of desolation, as they are present or absent. Water is easily understood as purification, renewal, life itself, and so it is used in baptism. Some religious theme apparently lies behind this passage, and the 'red rock' of line 25 is not just any rock. We wonder if red is the colour of the blood of Christ that was shed for us — or of the old 'red gold' of ancient times. Here Eliot appears to try to help us. He urges us to read *From Ritual to Romance* which will 'elucidate the difficulties of the poem much better than my notes can do.' Many readers have sought Jessie Weston's book, for years obtainable only in large reference libraries, to be disappointed when they read it. Yet some notion of what that book is about we must have. The rock may be in part a reference to the Holy Grail, which was made of gold and held the red blood from the crucifixion. All of us know that there was a Quest for it — so it must have been lost — and that the land would not prosper until it was found. Most of us know that it was supposed to be the cup that was used at the Last Supper and later to catch the blood of the dying Christ and to have been brought to Glastonbury, still a cult centre after two millennia. We are likely to be *more* aware than Eliot's first readers that modern anthropology has found much interest in what used to be thought of as fairy stories: very ancient beliefs survive in ritualised forms (familiar to all Roman Catholics in the symbolic sacrifice of the Mass) and Arthurian legend, of which the Grail story is a part, has been scanned not only as a source of information about late Roman Britain, but as a link with far older things. The Grail and Spear may be stylised symbols of the sexes, representing their characteristic organs: the theme of fertility and renewal set against contemporary, post-war desolation is Eliot's own extension of that symbolism. An awareness of this stratum of meaning will help us towards the end of the poem, where it recurs — 'Here is no water but only rock' (l.331) — as will knowing the story of the betrayal in the garden of Gethsemane, which is clearly the foundation of the first part of 'What the Thunder said'.

We have spoken of one theme being set against another, and it is an appreciation of this as a technique that may well prove to be more helpful to us than anything else. From beginning to end, the poem invites us to draw parallels, to make comparisons between the desolate land seeking the Grail, its promise of renewal; the winter landscape yearning for spring; the primitive country of the Fisher King with its failing monarch reflecting its own barrenness; between Western Christianity, Christ with his nails who will 'dig ... up again' (l.75) the troubled conscience of Europe, the Hanged Man of the Tarot pack, the 'agony in stony places' (l.324), St Augustine who came to Carthage (l.307) — and Eastern mysticism, the Hindu interpretation of the sound of thunder from the Upanishads, the sermon on purifying fire preached by Buddha; above all, between past and present.

The poem continually invites us to make this comparison: the very opening puts the pre-war international jet set against the vision of the 'stony rubbish' of ruined, post-war Europe, to which we may add our own layer of meaning from the bomb-blasted cities of a later war. The crowd flowing over London Bridge (l.62) is seen as dying every day in the appalled words of Dante when he first saw the kingdom of the lost and realised how vast it was. The ancient sea-battle of Mylae, fought largely for economic reasons, becomes every battle. In 'A Game of Chess' the device is at its clearest. The allusions to Enobarbus's famous speech in *Antony and Cleopatra*, which gives a gorgeous

ption of the Queen as Antony first saw her, recall a world
ich adultery is carried out with style, vitality, and without
guilt. In contrast, the poem's rich bitch picks away at her lover
still haunted by his wartime experiences in 'rats' alley' and
hides from the real world in her closed car. This is the Roaring
Twenties in all its expensive selfishness. Lil, on the other hand,
is thirty-one, toothless already, ignorant of contraception, with
five children and a do-it-yourself abortion — poor Lil is one of
the lucky ones. Her man went right through the war ('He's been
in the army four years', l.148) and survived. The modern world
is morally idiotic, like the teller of this section, making no
distinction between Lil's dreadful plight and the importance of
eating gammon while it is hot. In the background the ominous
voice of the bar-tender calling for time suggests a situation
which cannot last much longer.

Similarly, in 'The Fire Sermon' the beautiful music of
Spenser's marriage poem contrasts with the polluted stream of
contemporary 'nymphs' or the ungainly and routine couplings
of Sweeney and Mrs Porter; while Mr Eugenides brings the
Glory that was Greece up to date in a grubby and dubious trader
with his ambiguous offers of weekends, himself, perhaps,
included; and Tiresias, a figure from the most searing of the
dramas of the ancient world, is brought in to witness the loveless spasm of an arrogant young womaniser and a girl who could
not live on her typist's salary but wanted to be independent, and
saw her virginity as something disposable. Copulation in a
canoe, a grotesque enough business in itself, is presented
against another sixteenth-century parallel, Elizabeth in her
state barge with her resplendent admirer, the Earl of Leicester,
while in the background from another time and culture,
Wagner's Rhine-maidens bewail the loss of their precious gold.
Then from the first great mercantile race, the Phoenicians, we
pass the Mount of Olives to a picture of a modern refugees'
Europe — 'hooded hordes swarming/ Over endless plains'
(ll.368–369) — and in a list of five names (to which we might
now add New York, Moscow and Peking) we are made to see
that every great civilisation lasts only a moment in the perspective of eternity. The poem ends with a handful of allusions from
many periods and cultures, thrown at us as some sort of emerg-
ency survival kit. We say we know more than people did in the

past. The past is what we know. To begin to grasp Eliot's poem, the one thing we need above all else is some sense of what has gone before us as a means of seeing more clearly what is around us now.

We began this study by supposing a student looking at the opening of the poem, and by suggesting the difficulty that the author himself felt in writing it. It may help us to conclude by looking at the end — lines 399–422 — and trying to decide how far he resolved it for us, ignorant as we are of so much that he took for granted.

With our layman's knowledge and our awareness of Eliot's method, we have no difficulty in identifying the holy Ganges, and we know that India is breathless and anxious before the monsoon breaks — if it does. Thunder makes loud booming sounds in which we can easily fancy we hear words. The three words in Sanskrit, a language to which our own is related, are translated for us as 'give, sympathise, control' in the Notes. These are orders, each of them presented to us in a picture. Most of us know that it is immensely hard to 'surrender', to expose ourselves completely to another person, to God, but it is only by such demanding contacts, such committal, that we achieve immortality: the comically traditional picture of the solicitor opening our will shows us how little our material life and possessions really mean, how briefly they last. We are then asked to sympathise, to share the sorrows of the world, loneliness in particular. We may not know, as Eliot did, the ghastly story of Ugolino and the tower locked up for ever, but we all know that we are locked up in our own skulls — 'each in his prison' — and that our only escape is in trying to respond to the loneliness of others, to their suffering, to their love. To try to exert some control over our wayward impulses, over the erratic and often awful courses of human behaviour, is surely our duty, and here Eliot's 'objective correlative' for this, the image of the small boat in the hands of an expert, speaks very loudly to me, as I am terrified of small boats and cannot control them. It probably works just as well with those who are 'expert with sail and oar'.

We can go on from this point, and on and on. We can learn that these three phases may represent three kinds of love: that of Eros, sexual love; that of the love-feast, the Agape, the

Communion, love of our fellows; and that of Charis, the unselfish love of God towards undeserving man. We can, if we wish, read all the Notes, and the many, many notes on the Notes. I hope, however, that we have discovered that, with a few simple ideas to guide us, we need no guide at all to begin our endless journey. Cyril Connolly said 'We should read it every April', and experience (so far) suggests that that is not a bad rule.

# AFTERTHOUGHTS

**1**

What do you understand by the term 'objective correlative' (page 118)?

**2**

Can *The Waste Land* be appreciated by someone with no knowledge of classical literature?

**3**

Why does Cunningham claim that 'allusion' is 'a key word in the study of Eliot' (page 119)?

**4**

Should *The Waste Land* be set for examinations?

**Cedric Watts**

*Cedric Watts is Professor of English at Sussex University, and author of many scholarly publications.*

ESSAY

# The last 10½ lines of *The Waste Land*

One easy way of dealing with the difficulties of *The Waste Land* is to condemn the whole poem as 'élitist' and stroll away from it looking politically self-righteous. That's also a daft way of dealing with them, given that much good poetry is cogently difficult: the poet, by subverting clichés of language, is disrupting some of our clichés of thought and feeling. New kinds of expression permit new kinds of experience. The great innovators in modern jazz — Gillespie, Parker, Monk — seemed difficult (and possibly 'élitist') to listeners who were attuned only to the clichés of traditional jazz. Elites aren't necessarily a bad thing: after all, Ian Botham belongs to an élite of highly skilled cricketers; and if we enter a doctor's surgery we expect to be treated by a qualified practitioner and not by a layman picked at random from the street.

A more industrious way of dealing with the difficulties of the poem is to trace the allusions and show how they fit together in a logical thematic and argumentative sequence. The snag with this approach is that it makes *The Waste Land* seem more rational than it is. The poem is a big paradox — irrationality challenges and is challenged by rationality — and by overemphasising the rationality the commentator may halve and kill the paradox.

Some of the obscurities are certainly misjudgements on Eliot's part: the punctuation is hit-and-miss, and sometimes the poet has needlessly omitted from the line-endings various punctuation marks that the syntax obliges us to supply. But, most of the time, the difficulties seem to be a necessary part of the poem's meaning: our sense of resistance, of our struggle to decipher recalcitrant materials, embodies one of the poem's main implications. For this is a poem about the struggle to find meaning within the apparently chaotic and senseless; a struggle at a personal level, within an individual trying to come to terms with despair, disgust, boredom, neurosis and madness; and a struggle at a historic level, by a poet striving to record, reflect and interpret the sense that the modern period (and not simply the immediate aftermath of the First World War) is a period of apparent disintegration. *The Waste Land* is at once very private and very public. It says 'What shall we do to be saved?', yet remains fascinated by perdition — by loss and the lost; it zealously enacts the breakdown for which it seeks a cure. And it remains a craftily critic-proof poem, because it anticipates and answers most of the critical objections it subsequently incurred. 'Obscure'? So were the Sybil's prophecies. 'Arduous'? So was the quest for the Holy Grail. 'Misanthropic'? So seems much good satire.

I'm going to illustrate the paradox of the simultaneous celebration of rationality and irrationality by looking closely at the poem's final ten-and-a-half lines. Here they are:

I sat upon the shore
Fishing, with the arid plain behind me
Shall I at least set my lands in order?
London Bridge is falling down falling down falling down
*Poi s'ascose nel foco che gli affina*
*Quando fiam uti chelidon* — O swallow swallow
*Le Prince d'Aquitaine à la tour abolie*
These fragments I have shored against my ruins
Why then Ile fit you. Hieronymo's mad againe.
Datta. Dayadhvam, Damyata.
Shantih shantih shantih

I'll do the rationalist's job in a minute; but let's begin with first impressions of those lines — with gut-responses, reflex-responses. My first impression, when I read them or hear them, is of madness. Stark raving lunacy. Hieronymo's mad againe, and so's the narrator. If someone came up to me in the street talking like that, I'd cross the road fast to get away from him. Another thing: listening to that passage is like being taken on a sprint through the Tower of Babel. There's a Babelish babble of different voices and languages. I think that the biblical story (Genesis 11:1–9) of the Tower of Babel provided one of Eliot's themes. The builders were presumptuous, so God thwarted and punished them by making them all talk different languages, and they couldn't understand each other.

You may feel, on the other hand, that listening to that passage is less like a sprint through Babel than like listening to a radio while someone else rapidly twirls the wavelength knob so that we pick up a medley of different stations: London, Rome, Paris, Delhi; snatches of talks, of poems, of plays, of sermons, of music. The ideal rendering of *The Waste Land* wouldn't be a one-person recitation. It would be a radio programme which uses a variety of readers, singers and actors; which turns some parts into sermons and others into plays; which has an immense number of sound-effects: Wagnerian orchestral passages with opera-singers when Wagner is being quoted, an Australian pub chorus when the Mrs Porter ballad appears. And, in that final sequence, the 'London Bridge is falling down' line would be sung by children recorded in a park or playground. The whole thing makes an exuberant sonic mishmash.

The rationalist's way of dealing with the passage is to emphasise its internal logic and its logical connections with what has gone before. The first three parts of *The Waste Land* dramatised a series of interlinked problems, personal, social, cultural and historical, which could all be summed up in that one question: What can I — and we — do to be saved? (Saved from boredom, neurosis, breakdown; from a sense of sterility and confusion and meaninglessness?) The fourth part, on Phlebas the Phoenician, provided a reminder of mortality and the suggestion of a purifying transition or sea-change. At the fifth part, 'What the Thunder said', the poem seems to be struggling erratically towards some revelation or answer to the dominant question. There's imagery of oppressive drought and sterility; but we're reminded that after the crucifixion of Jesus, two of his despondent disciples, journeying to Emmaus, were actually accompanied for a time by the risen Christ but failed to recognise him; the suggestion is that salvation may be close at hand when it seems to be farthest away. (The disciples were slow to decode experience.) Then, in the desert, a mirage or hallucination: a surrealistic doomsday vision of hooded hordes, of the collapse of a city or cities; more apocalyptic visions mixing biblical allusions (imprisonment of John the Baptist; the drought described by Jeremiah) with images of madness and hellishness. Next, amid mountains, an empty decaying chapel. Perhaps this suggests simply the want of religious faith in modern times, but it's also a particular reference (Eliot's Notes say) to the Chapel Perilous where the knight who was questing for the Grail had to undergo various ordeals before completing his quest. Then we're conveyed to the Himalayas, where the thunder speaks, and it says 'DA'. That syllable looks pretty inadequate on paper, even in capitals. In a radio production you could have the actual sound of thunder blended with a booming God-like voice saying 'DA'. Eliot's very useful footnote tells us that he's referring to one of the Sanskrit holy texts, the Upanishads. If you look up the particular Upanishad he cites, you find that the Babel theme is being maintained: one day, gods, men and demons all called on the Lord Almighty to speak to them, and when he replied 'Da', each group naturally interpreted this cryptic remark in a different way. One group took it to be *Datta*, meaning 'Give' (be charitable); another took it to be *Dayadhvam*, meaning 'Sympathise' (have compassion); and another took it to be *Damyata*, meaning 'Control yourselves'. (The interpretations differed, yet each conveyed part of the message.) All right; these teachings sound reasonable and familiar. So why has Eliot gone to the trouble of dragging in Sanskrit? Why couldn't he use plain English? If it has to be the voice of the Lord, why couldn't he have *Jesus* saying you need faith, hope and charity?

One reason is that this poem makes us enact the struggle to extract meaning from what appears meaningless. *The Waste Land* is a poem in code; its coded message is that life's senselessness contains a meaning to be decoded. The poem enacts what it claims the world is: a problem implying a solution. The Hindu message, when we decipher it, resembles a Christian message; and the resemblance hints that if different religious systems at different times and places have made similar recommendations, perhaps that shows they have common wisdom; perhaps even a common divine source. Notice that Eliot is cunningly turning upside down the argument of Sir James Frazer's *The Golden Bough*. Frazer had attacked Christianity by saying that it wasn't unique; it resembled many pagan beliefs about a dying and rising god, and all had their origin in fertility-rituals, in the human need for a full belly. Eliot reverses Frazer by saying that if there are common features in different religious systems, there's no smoke without fire: perhaps they all, in diverse ways, testify to the existence of the divine.

Nevertheless, after the doctrinal clarification offered by the 'Datta, Dayadhvam, Damyata' section, the poem pauses, and then:

> I sat upon the shore
> Fishing, with the arid plain behind me
> Shall I at least set my lands in order?

The effect is almost one of bathos, of anticlimax. There's a sudden scaling-down or refocusing. The focus narrows to a solitary figure in the foreground, fishing, with arid plains behind him. So the long-promised rain hasn't fallen. If he's fishing for final truth, he hasn't yet caught anything after all. The effect is like an awakening after a dream-vision; and the narrator fleetingly resembles the maimed impotent Fisher King of the Grail legends who lives in a waste land waiting for a time when some redemption may come. 'Shall I at least set my lands in order?' perhaps means 'I can't set the *world* to rights, but I may be able to make the best of my own little *corner* of it'. There's another biblical allusion here, to King Hezekiah, the ailing monarch who was told by Isaiah to set his lands in order; who did so and was blessed by God. So there's a faint note of hope. The next line is 'London Bridge is falling down falling down falling down'. If you go tone-deaf and pedantic at this point, you can say that this line echoes the theme of the decay and destruction of civilisations. Yet London Bridge was rebuilt; and in any case that's much too solemn a gloss. Eliot is quoting a song sung down the generations by children happily at play. A phase of decay has become commemorated in a lyric of youthful innocence; disaster can become an occasion of joy through song. *The Waste Land* is about metamorphoses: healing transformations as well as grim breakdowns.

Next line: '*Poi s'ascose nel foco che gli affina*'. The speaker is Dante, in Purgatorio, canto 26. The line means 'Then he hid in the fire that refines them'. The 'he' is Arnaut Daniel, the medieval Provençal poet. He has just told Dante that he repents the sins of his past and looks forward to the heaven that he will eventually reach after suffering the purgatorial flames. Perhaps our *Waste Land* poet will be able, encouraged by the example of Daniel, to bear his own private purgatory. '*Quando fiam uti chelidon*' means 'When shall I be like the swallow?' It's a line from the anonymous Latin poem 'Pervigilium Veneris', a hymn to Venus and a celebration of the spring and love. The Latin writer says that the ravished Philomela has become a bird and her complaints sound as joyous song. One function of this allusion is that it completes the sequence of references to Philomela, the victim of sexual lust, who was also an instance of healing metamorphosis, being transformed into a songbird. The following phrase, 'O swallow swallow', refers to Tennyson's lyric in *The Princess*: that swallow is flying south, to warm lands, away from the earthbound poet: another reminder of the bird's power to soar and sing spontaneously.

Next line: '*Le Prince d'Aquitaine à la tour abolie*'. It means: 'The Prince of Aquitaine at the ruined tower', a line from Nerval's 'El Desdichado' (The Unfortunate or Disinherited Man') — a French poem with a Spanish title. The gist of the poem is: 'I've been through hell, but I've survived to tell the tale; I've known loss and grief, but I've had my dreams and can make songs of my experiences.' The reference to the ruined tower leads naturally to Eliot's next line, 'These fragments I have shored against my ruins'. The narrator is telling us that these fragments of poetry called *The Waste Land* constitute a holding operation; they shore him up; they help him to ward off collapse. Next: 'Why then Ile fit you. Hieronymo's mad againe'. The last phrase is the subtitle of Thomas Kyd's play, *The*

*Spanish Tragedy*. Perhaps Eliot is mocking himself a little here: now that he's offering yet another flurry of telescoped quotations, perhaps people will think he's crazy, as they thought Hieronymo was in the play. But the other part of the line, 'Why then Ile fit you', offers a warning. The words mean 'Why, certainly I'll fix it for you'. What Hieronymo provides for the corrupt court is a revenge-drama in many tongues, during the performance of which real blood is shed, real revenge is taken on the villains. There was method in his madness. Eliot then repeats 'Datta. Dayadhvam. Damyata': the religious teaching is re-echoed. And finally, 'Shantih shantih shantih': Eliot translates it for us as 'The peace which passeth understanding', to help those who fear that his poem may be the piece which passeth understanding.

So *The Waste Land* is not only a poem which argues that a search for religious values can redeem the world from that loss of meaning and vitality which (allegedly) is the price of the secular outlook; it also obliges *us* to enact the quest to redeem the seemingly meaningless as we read the poem itself. Eliot implies that in life, as in the poem, the apparent meaninglessness may have been set before us as a challenge. If we look back on the numerous allusions crammed into the last ten-and-a-half lines of *The Waste Land*, we find that with a bit of nudging and elbowing they can be fitted together into a kind of testament; it declares: 'I've experienced my vision; perhaps there's light at the end of the tunnel; art offers consolations for woe; other artists have made song of suffering and used art to change the world; and if I can't sing at the moment I hope to in the future and my attempts at art are at least palliatives. Apparent madness can make a kind of sense; religious consolation offers a remote, obscure hope, but it will bear meditation and perhaps promises peace'.

But that's only half the paradox. The 'testament' does battle with its manner of utterance, its sound, feel and impact. After the relative lucidity and assurance of the Damyata lines about the boat and the controlling hands, it sounds as though there's a sudden veering away from assurance and lucidity into the cryptic, the confused and twittering; a regression from more public utterance to the more private and delphic. The narrator is partly recapitulating previous themes and preoccupations, partly sinking back into the medley and confusion of its echoing quotations and jumbled fragments. So, that ending is highly ambiguous and equivocal. It offers garbled hints of consolation, of hope, of peace, while the manner of the garbling suggests disorder, confusion and near-madness.

To conclude. If a critic complains, as Louis Untermeyer complained, that *The Waste Land* is merely a heap of 'flotsam and jetsam', perhaps he resembles the inadequate Grail-quester who failed to enquire the meaning of the symbols. If, on the other hand, the critic makes the poem sound like a fully ordered and intellectually stable work, he has underestimated the erratic mishmash of cacophanous sound-effects and surrealistic imagery. If he complains, as L G Salingar has complained, that Eliot presents too negative and pessimistic a picture of life, just ask such a critic how he proposes to deal with the satires of Juvenal, Ben Jonson, Pope and Swift, or with the modernist pessimism of Sartre and Beckett, or with the love of irrationality expressed by various recent literary theorists. In the words of Thomas Hardy:

> If way to the Better there be, it exacts a full look at the Worst.
>
> ('In Tenebris II')

# AFTERTHOUGHTS

## 1

What 'clichés of language' (see paragraph one) does *The Waste Land* subvert?

## 2

In what ways does Watts relate his consideration of the last $10\frac{1}{2}$ lines of *The Waste Land* to the concerns of the poem as a whole?

## 3

What do you understand by 'apocalyptic visions' (page 131)?

## 4

Do you agree with Watts's 'translation' of the ending of *The Waste Land* (page 134, lines 25–32)?

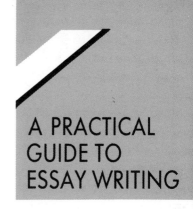

# A PRACTICAL GUIDE TO ESSAY WRITING

## INTRODUCTION

First, a word of warning. Good essays are the product of a creative engagement with literature. So never try to restrict your studies to what you think will be 'useful in the exam'. Ironically, you will restrict your grade potential if you do.

This doesn't mean, of course, that you should ignore the basic skills of essay writing. When you read critics, make a conscious effort to notice *how* they communicate their ideas. The guidelines that follow offer advice of a more explicit kind. But they are no substitute for practical experience. It is never easy to express ideas with clarity and precision. But the more often you tackle the problems involved and experiment to find your own voice, the more fluent you will become. So practise writing essays as often as possible.

# HOW TO PLAN
# AN ESSAY

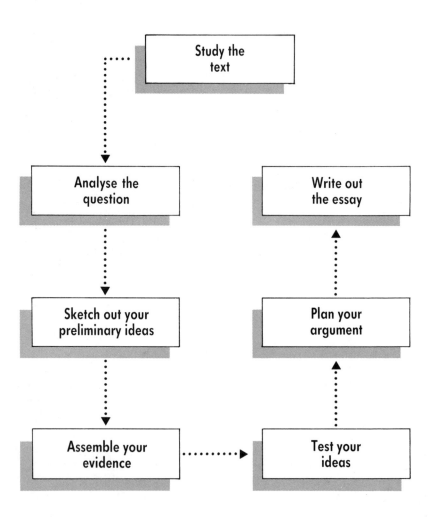

## Study the text

The first step in writing a good essay is to get to know the set text well. Never write about a text until you are fully familiar with it. Even a discussion of the opening chapter of a novel, for example, should be informed by an understanding of the book as a whole. Literary texts, however, are by their very nature complex and on a first reading you are bound to miss many significant features. Re-read the book with care, if possible more than once. Look up any unfamiliar words in a good dictionary and if the text you are studying was written more than a few decades ago, consult the *Oxford English Dictionary* to find out whether the meanings of any terms have shifted in the intervening period.

Good books are difficult to put down when you first read them. But a more leisurely second or third reading gives you the opportunity to make notes on those features you find significant. An index of characters and events is often useful, particularly when studying novels with a complex plot or time scheme. The main aim, however, should be to record your *responses* to the text. By all means note, for example, striking images. But be sure to add *why* you think them striking. Similarly, record any thoughts you may have on interesting comparisons with other texts, puzzling points of characterisation, even what you take to be aesthetic blemishes. The important thing is to annotate fully and adventurously. The most seemingly idiosyncratic comment may later lead to a crucial area of discussion which you would otherwise have overlooked. It helps to have a working copy of the text in which to mark up key passages and jot down marginal comments (although obviously these practices are taboo when working with library, borrowed or valuable copies!). But keep a fuller set of notes as well and organise these under appropriate headings.

Literature does not exist in an aesthetic vacuum, however, and you should try to find out as much as possible about the context of its production and reception. It is particularly important to read other works by the same author and writings by contemporaries. At this early stage, you may want to restrict your secondary reading to those standard reference works, such as biographies, which are widely available in public libraries. In the long run, however, it pays to read as wide a range of critical studies as possible.

Some students, and tutors, worry that such studies may stifle the development of any truly personal response. But this won't happen if you are alert to the danger and read critically. After all, you wouldn't passively accept what a stranger told you in conversation. The fact that a critic's views are in print does not necessarily make them any more authoritative (as a glance at the review pages of the *TLS* and *London Review of Books* will reveal). So question the views you find: 'Does this critic's interpretation agree with mine and where do we part company?' 'Can it be right to try and restrict this text's meanings to those found by its author or first audience?' 'Doesn't this passage treat a theatrical text as though it were a novel?' Often it is views which you reject which prove most valuable since they challenge you to articulate your own position with greater clarity. Be sure to keep careful notes on what the critic wrote, and your *reactions* to what the critic wrote.

## Analyse the question

You cannot begin to answer a question until you understand what task it is you have been asked to perform. Recast the question in your own words and reconstruct the line of reasoning which lies behind it. Where there is a choice of topics, try to choose the one for which you are best prepared. It would, for example, be unwise to tackle 'How far do you agree that in *Paradise Lost* Milton transformed the epic models he inherited from ancient Greece and Rome?' without a working knowledge of Homer and Virgil (or *Paradise Lost* for that matter!). If you do not already know the works of these authors, the question should spur you on to read more widely — or discourage you from attempting it at all. The scope of an essay, however, is not always so obvious and you must remain alert to the implied demands of each question. How could you possibly 'Consider the view that *Wuthering Heights* transcends the conventions of the Gothic novel' without reference to at least some of those works which, the question suggests, have *not* transcended Gothic conventions?

When you have decided on a topic, analyse the terms of the question itself. Sometimes these self-evidently require careful definition: *tragedy* and *irony*, for example, are notoriously difficult concepts to pin down and you will probably need to consult a good dictionary of literary terms. Don't ignore, however, those seemingly innocuous phrases which often smuggle in significant assumptions. 'Does Macbeth lack the nobility of the true tragic hero?' obviously invites you to discuss nobility and the nature of the tragic hero. But what of 'lack' and 'true' — do they suggest that the play would be improved had Shakespeare depicted Macbeth in a different manner? or that tragedy is superior to other forms of drama? Remember that you are not expected meekly to agree with the assumptions implicit in the question. Some questions are deliberately provocative in order to stimulate an engaged response. Don't be afraid to take up the challenge.

## Sketch out your preliminary ideas

'Which comes first, the evidence or the answer?' is one of those chicken and egg questions. How can you form a view without inspecting the evidence? But how can you know which evidence is relevant without some idea of what it is you are looking for? In practice the mind reviews evidence and formulates preliminary theories or hypotheses at one and the same time, although for the sake of clarity we have separated out the processes. Remember that these early ideas are only there to get you started. You *expect* to modify them in the light of the evidence you uncover. Your initial hypothesis may be an instinctive 'gut-reaction'. Or you may find that you prefer to 'sleep on the problem', allowing ideas to gell over a period of time. Don't worry in either case. The mind is quite capable of processing a vast amount of accumulated evidence, the product of previous reading and thought, and reaching sophisticated intuitive judgements. Eventually, however, you are going to have to think carefully through any ideas you arrive at by such intuitive processes. Are they logical? Do they take account of all the relevant factors? Do they fully answer the question set? Are there any obvious reasons to qualify or abandon them?

## Assemble your evidence

Now is the time to return to the text and re-read it with the question and your working hypothesis firmly in mind. Many of the notes you have already made are likely to be useful, but assess the precise relevance of this material and make notes on any new evidence you discover. The important thing is to cast your net widely and take into account points which tend to undermine your case as well as those that support it. As always, ensure that your notes are full, accurate, and reflect your own critical judgements.

You may well need to go outside the text if you are to do full justice to the question. If you think that the 'Oedipus complex' may be relevant to an answer on *Hamlet* then read Freud and a balanced selection of those critics who have discussed the appropriateness of applying psychoanalytical theories to the interpretation of literature. Their views can most easily be tracked down by consulting the annotated bibliographies held by most major libraries (and don't be afraid to ask a librarian for help in finding and using these). Remember that you go to works of criticism not only to obtain information but to stimulate you into clarifying your own position. And that since life is short and many critical studies are long, judicious use of a book's index and/or contents list is not to be scorned. You can save yourself a great deal of future labour if you carefully record full bibliographic details at this stage.

Once you have collected the evidence, organise it coherently. Sort the detailed points into related groups and identify the quotations which support these. You must also assess the relative importance of each point, for in an essay of limited length it is essential to establish a firm set of priorities, exploring some ideas in depth while discarding or subordinating others.

## Test your ideas

As we stressed earlier, a hypothesis is only a proposal, and one that you fully expect to modify. Review it with the evidence before you. Do you really still believe in it? It would be surprising if you did not want to modify it in some way. If you cannot see any problems, others may. Try discussing your ideas with friends and relatives. Raise them in class discussions. Your tutor is certain to welcome your initiative. The critical process is essentially collaborative and there is absolutely no reason why you should not listen to and benefit from the views of others. Similarly, you should feel free to test your ideas against the theories put forward in academic journals and books. But do not just borrow what you find. Critically analyse the views on offer and, where appropriate, integrate them into your own pattern of thought. You must, of course, give full acknowledgement to the sources of such views.

Do not despair if you find you have to abandon or modify significantly your initial position. The fact that you are prepared to do so is a mark of intellectual integrity. Dogmatism is never an academic virtue and many of the best essays explore the *process* of scholarly enquiry rather than simply record its results.

## Plan your argument

Once you have more or less decided on your attitude to the question (for an answer is never really 'finalised') you have to present your case in the most persuasive manner. In order to do this you must avoid meandering from point to point and instead produce an organised argument — a structured flow of ideas and supporting evidence, leading logically to a conclusion which fully answers the question. Never begin to write until you have produced an outline of your argument.

You may find it easiest to begin by sketching out its main stage as a flow chart or some other form of visual presentation. But eventually you should produce a list of paragraph topics. The paragraph is the conventional written demarcation for a unit of thought and you can outline an argument quite simply by briefly summarising the substance of each paragraph and then checking that these points (you may remember your English teacher referring to them as topic sentences) really do follow a coherent order. Later you will be able to elaborate on each topic, illustrating and qualifying it as you go along. But you will find this far easier to do if you possess from the outset a clear map of where you are heading.

All questions require some form of an argument. Even so-called 'descriptive' questions *imply* the need for an argument. An adequate answer to the request to 'Outline the role of Iago in *Othello*' would do far more than simply list his appearances on stage. It would at the very least attempt to provide some *explanation* for his actions — is he, for example, a representative stage 'Machiavel'? an example of pure evil, 'motiveless malignity'? or a realistic study of a tormented personality reacting to identifiable social and psychological pressures?

Your conclusion ought to address the terms of the question. It may seem obvious, but 'how far do you agree', 'evaluate', 'consider', 'discuss', etc, are *not* interchangeable formulas and your conclusion must take account of the precise wording of the question. If asked 'How far do you agree?', the concluding paragraph of your essay really should state whether you are in complete agreement, total disagreement, or, more likely, partial agreement. Each preceding paragraph should have a clear justification for its existence and help to clarify the reasoning which underlies your conclusion. If you find that a paragraph serves no good purpose (perhaps merely summarising the plot), do not hesitate to discard it.

The arrangement of the paragraphs, the overall strategy of the argument, can vary. One possible pattern is dialectical: present the arguments in favour of one point of view (**thesis**); then turn to counter-arguments or to a rival interpretation (**antithesis**); finally evaluate the competing claims and arrive at your own conclusion (**synthesis**). You may, on the other hand, feel so convinced of the merits of one particular case that you wish to devote your entire essay to arguing that viewpoint persuasively (although it is always desirable to indicate, however briefly, that you are aware of alternative, if flawed, positions). As the essays contained in this volume demonstrate, there are many other possible strategies. Try to adopt the one which will most comfortably accommodate the demands of the question and allow you to express your thoughts with the greatest possible clarity.

Be careful, however, not to apply abstract formulas in a mechanical manner. It is true that you should be careful to define your terms. It is *not* true that every essay should begin with 'The dictionary defines $x$ as ...'. In fact, definitions are often best left until an appropriate moment for their introduction arrives. Similarly every essay should have a beginning, middle and end. But it does not follow that in your opening paragraph you should announce an intention to write an essay, or that in your concluding paragraph you need to signal an imminent desire to put down your pen. The old adages are often useful reminders of what constitutes good practice, but they must be interpreted intelligently.

## Write out the essay

Once you have developed a coherent argument you should aim to communicate it in the most effective manner possible. Make certain you clearly identify yourself, and the question you are answering. Ideally, type your answer, or at least ensure your handwriting is legible and that you leave sufficient space for your tutor's comments. Careless presentation merely distracts from the force of your argument. Errors of grammar, syntax and spelling are far more serious. At best they are an irritating blemish, particularly in the work of a student who should be sensitive to the nuances of language. At worst, they seriously confuse the sense of your argument. If you are aware that you have stylistic problems of this kind, ask your tutor for advice at the earliest opportunity. Everyone, however, is liable to commit the occasional howler. The only remedy is to give yourself plenty of time in which to proof-read your manuscript (often reading it aloud is helpful) before submitting it.

Language, however, is not only an instrument of communication; it is also an instrument of thought. If you want to think clearly and precisely you should strive for a clear, precise prose style. Keep your sentences short and direct. Use modern, straightforward English wherever possible. Avoid repetition, clichés and wordiness. Beware of generalisations, simplifications, and overstatements. Orwell analysed the relationship between stylistic vice and muddled thought in his essay 'Politics and the English Language' (1946) — it remains essential reading (and is still readily available in volume 4 of the Penguin *Collected Essays, Journalism and Letters*). Generalisations, for example, are always dangerous. They are rarely true and tend to suppress the individuality of the texts in question. A remark such as 'Keats always employs sensuous language in his poetry' is not only fatuous (what, after all, does it mean? is *every* word he wrote equally 'sensuous'?) but tends to obscure interesting distinctions which could otherwise be made between, say, the descriptions in the 'Ode on a Grecian Urn' and those in 'To Autumn'.

The intelligent use of quotations can help you make your points with greater clarity. Don't sprinkle them throughout your essay without good reason. There is no need, for example, to use them to support uncontentious statements of fact. 'Macbeth murdered Duncan' does not require textual evidence (unless you wish to dispute Thurber's brilliant parody, 'The Great Macbeth Murder Mystery', which reveals Lady Macbeth's father as the culprit!). Quotations should be included, however, when they are necessary to support your case. The proposition that Macbeth's imaginative powers wither after he has killed his king would certainly require extensive quotation: you would almost certainly want to analyse key passages from both before and after the murder (perhaps his first and last soliloquies?). The key word here is 'analyse'. Quotations cannot make your points on their own. It is up to you to demonstrate their relevance and clearly explain to your readers *why* you want them to focus on the passage you have selected.

Most of the academic conventions which govern the presentation of essays are set out briefly in the style sheet below. The question of gender, however, requires fuller discussion. More than half the population of the world is female. Yet many writers still refer to an undifferentiated *man*kind. Or write of the author and *his* public. We do not think that this convention has much to recommend it. At the very least, it runs the risk of introducing unintended sexist attitudes. And at times leads to such patent absurdities as 'Cleopatra's final speech asserts *man*'s true nobility'. With a little thought, you can normally find ways of expressing yourself which do not suggest that the typical author, critic or reader is male. Often you can simply use plural forms, which is probably a more elegant solution than relying on such awkward formulations as 's/he' or 'he and she'. You should also try to avoid distinguishing between male and female authors on the basis of forenames. Why *Jane* Austen and not *George* Byron? Refer to all authors by their last names unless there is some good reason not to. Where there may otherwise be confusion, say between T S and George Eliot, give the name in full when it first occurs and thereafter use the last name only.

Finally, keep your audience firmly in mind. Tutors and examiners are interested in understanding your conclusions and the processes by which you arrived at them. They are not interested in reading a potted version of a book they already know. **So don't pad out your work with plot summary.**

## Hints for examinations

In an examination you should go through exactly the same processes as you would for the preparation of a term essay. The only difference lies in the fact that some of the stages will have had to take place before you enter the examination room. This should not bother you unduly. Examiners are bound to avoid the merely eccentric when they come to formulate papers and if you have read widely and thought deeply about the central issues raised by your set texts you can be confident you will have sufficient material to answer the majority of questions sensibly.

The fact that examinations impose strict time limits makes it *more* rather than less, important that you plan carefully. There really is no point in floundering into an answer without any idea of where you are going, particularly when there will not be time to recover from the initial error.

Before you begin to answer any question at all, study the entire paper with care. Check that you understand the rubric and know how many questions you have to answer and whether any are compulsory. It may be comforting to spot a title you feel confident of answering well, but don't rush to tackle it: read *all* the questions before deciding which *combination* will allow you to display your abilities to the fullest advantage. Once you have made your choice, analyse each question, sketch out your ideas, assemble the evidence, review your initial hypothesis, play your argument, *before* trying to write out an answer. And make notes at each stage: not only will these help you arrive at a sensible conclusion, but examiners are impressed by evidence of careful thought.

Plan your time as well as your answers. If you have practised writing timed essays as part of your revision, you should not find this too difficult. There can be a temptation to allocate extra time to the questions you know you can answer well; but this is always a short-sighted policy. You will find yourself left to face a question which would in any event have given you difficulty without even the time to give it serious thought. It is, moreover, easier to gain marks at the lower end of the scale than at the upper, and you will never compensate for one poor answer by further polishing two satisfactory answers. Try to leave some time at the end of the examination to re-read your answers and correct any obvious errors. If the worst comes to the worst and you run short of time, don't just keep writing until you are forced to break off in mid-paragraph. It is far better to provide for the examiner a set of notes which indicate the overall direction of your argument.

Good luck — but if you prepare for the examination conscientiously and tackle the paper in a methodical manner, you won't need it!

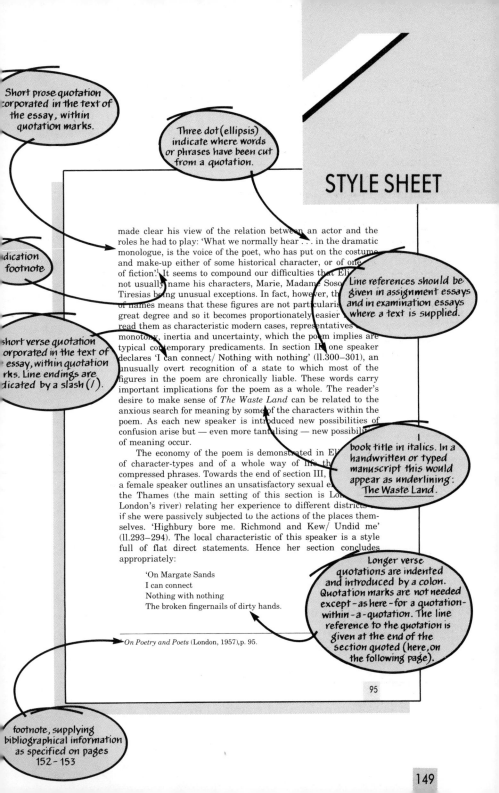

**Short prose quotation incorporated in the text of the essay, within quotation marks.**

**Three dot (ellipsis) indicate where words or phrases have been cut from a quotation.**

**dication footnote**

**short verse quotation orporated in the text of essay, within quotation rks. Line endings are dicated by a slash (/).**

**Line references should be given in assignment essays and in examination essays where a text is supplied.**

**book title in italics. In a handwritten or typed manuscript this would appear as underlining: The Waste Land.**

**Longer verse quotations are indented and introduced by a colon. Quotation marks are not needed except - as here - for a quotation-within-a-quotation. The line reference to the quotation is given at the end of the section quoted (here, on the following page).**

**footnote, supplying bibliographical information as specified on pages 152 - 153**

made clear his view of the relation between an actor and the roles he had to play: 'What we normally hear . . . in the dramatic monologue, is the voice of the poet, who has put on the costume and make-up either of some historical character, or of one of fiction'. It seems to compound our difficulties that Eli not usually name his characters, Marie, Madame Soso Tiresias being unusual exceptions. In fact, however, th of names means that these figures are not particularis great degree and so it becomes proportionately easier read them as characteristic modern cases, representatives monotony, inertia and uncertainty, which the poem implies are typical contemporary predicaments. In section III one speaker declares 'I can connect/ Nothing with nothing' (ll.300–301), an unusually overt recognition of a state to which most of the figures in the poem are chronically liable. These words carry important implications for the poem as a whole. The reader's desire to make sense of *The Waste Land* can be related to the anxious search for meaning by some of the characters within the poem. As each new speaker is introduced new possibilities of confusion arise but — even more tantalising — new possibili of meaning occur.

The economy of the poem is demonstrated in El of character-types and of a whole way of life th compressed phrases. Towards the end of section III, a female speaker outlines an unsatisfactory sexual e the Thames (the main setting of this section is Lo London's river) relating her experience to different districts if she were passively subjected to the actions of the places them-selves. 'Highbury bore me. Richmond and Kew/ Undid me' (ll.293–294). The local characteristic of this speaker is a style full of flat direct statements. Hence her section concludes appropriately:

> 'On Margate Sands
> I can connect
> Nothing with nothing
> The broken fingernails of dirty hands.

---

*On Poetry and Poets* (London, 1957),p. 95.

95

149

We have divided the following information into two sections. Part A describes those rules which it is essential to master no matter what kind of essay you are writing (including examination answers). Part B sets out some of the more detailed conventions which govern the documentation of essays.

# PART A: LAYOUT

## Titles of texts

**Titles of published books**, plays (of any length), long poems, pamphlets and periodicals (including newspapers and magazines), works of classical literature, and films should be underlined: e.g. David Copperfield (novel), Twelfth Night (play), Paradise Lost (long poem), Critical Quarterly (periodical), Horace's Ars Poetica (Classical work), Apocalypse Now (film).

Notice how important it is to distinguish between titles and other names. Hamlet is the play; Hamlet the prince. Wuthering Heights is the novel; Wuthering Heights the house. Underlining is the equivalent in handwritten or typed manuscripts of printed italics. So what normally appears in this volume as *Othello* would be written as Othello in your essay.

**Titles of articles**, essays, short stories, short poems, songs, chapters of books, speeches, and newspaper articles are enclosed in quotation marks; e.g. 'The Flea' (short poem), 'The Prussian Officer' (short story), 'Middleton's Chess Strategies' (article), 'Thatcher Defects!' (newspaper headline).

**Exceptions**: Underlining titles or placing them within quotation marks does not apply to sacred writings (e.g. Bible, Koran, Old Testament, Gospels) or parts of a book (e.g. Preface, Introduction, Appendix).

It is generally incorrect to place quotation marks around a title of a published book which you have underlined. The exception is 'titles within titles': e.g. 'Vanity Fair: A Critical Study (title of a book about *Vanity Fair*).

## Quotations

**Short verse quotations** of a single line or part of a line should be incorporated within quotation marks as part of the running text of your essay. Quotations of two or three lines of verse are treated in the same way, with line endings indicated by a slash(/). For example:

1   In <u>Julius Caesar</u>, Antony says of Brutus, 'This was the noblest Roman of them all'.
2   The opening of Antony's famous funeral oration, 'Friends, Romans, Countrymen, lend me your ears;/ I come to bury Caesar not to praise him', is a carefully controlled piece of rhetoric.

**Longer verse quotations** of more than three lines should be indented from the main body of the text and introduced in most cases with a colon. Do not enclose indented quotations within quotation marks. For example:
It is worth pausing to consider the reasons Brutus gives to justify his decision to assassinate Caesar:

> It must be by his death; and for my part,
> I know no personal cause to spurn at him,
> But for the general. He would be crowned.
> How might that change his nature, there's the question.

At first glance his rationale may appear logical . . .

**Prose quotations** of less than three lines should be incorporated in the text of the essay, within quotation marks. Longer prose quotations should be indented and the quotation marks omitted. For example:

1   Before his downfall, Caesar rules with an iron hand. His political opponents, the Tribunes Marullus and Flavius, are 'put to silence' for the trivial offence of 'pulling scarfs off Caesar's image'.
2   It is interesting to note the rhetorical structure of Brutus's Forum speech:

> Romans, countrymen, and lovers, hear me for my cause, and be silent that you may hear. Believe me for my honour, and have respect to mine honour that you may believe. Censure me in your wisdom, and awake your senses, that you may the better judge.

**Tenses**: When you are relating the events that occur within a work of fiction or describing the author's technique, it is the convention to use the present tense. Even though Orwell published *Animal Farm* in 1945, the book *describes* the animals' seizure of Manor Farm. Similarly, Macbeth always *murders* Duncan, despite the passage of time.

# PART B: DOCUMENTATION

**When quoting from verse** of more than twenty lines, provide line references: e.g. In 'Upon Appleton House' Marvell's mower moves 'With whistling scythe and elbow strong' (l.393).

**Quotations from plays** should be identified by act, scene and line references: e.g. Prospero, in Shakespeare's The Tempest, refers to Caliban as 'A devil, a born devil' (IV.1.188). (i.e. Act 4. Scene 1. Line 188).

**Quotations from prose** works should provide a chapter reference and, where appropriate, a page reference.

**Bibliographies** should list full details of all sources consulted. The way is which they are presented varies, but one standard format is as follows:

1  Books and articles are listed in alphabetical order by the author's last name. Initials are placed after the surname.
2  If you are referring to a chapter or article within a larger work, you list it by reference to the author of the article or chapter, not the editor (although the editor is also named in the reference).
3  Give (in parentheses) the place and date of publication, e.g. (London, 1962). These details can be found within the book itself. Here are some examples:

> Brockbank, J. P., 'Shakespeare's Histories, English and Roman', in Ricks, C. (ed.) English Drama to 1710 (Sphere History of Literature in the English Language) (London, 1971).
>
> Gurr, A., 'Richard III and the Democratic Process', Essays in Criticism 24 (1974), pp. 39–47.
>
> Spivack, B., Shakespeare and the Allegory of Evil (New York, 1958).

**Footnotes**: In general, try to avoid using footnotes and build your references into the body of the essay wherever possible. When you do use them give the full bibliographic reference to a work in the first instance and then use a short title: e.g. See K. Smidt, <u>Unconformities in Shakespeare's History Plays</u> (London, 1982), pp. 43–47 becomes Smidt (pp. 43–47) thereafter. Do not use terms such as 'ibid.' or 'op. cit.' unless you are absolutely sure of their meaning.

There is a principle behind all this seeming pedantry. The reader ought to be able to find and check your references and quotations as quickly and easily as possible. Give additional information, such as canto or volume number whenever you think it will assist your reader.

# SUGGESTIONS FOR FURTHER READING

**Biography**
Ackroyd, P, *T. S. Eliot* (London, 1984)

**Works by T S Eliot**
'*The Waste Land': A Facsimile and Transcript*, ed. Valerie Eliot
(London, 1971)
*Collected Poems 1909–1962* (London, 1963)
*Selected Prose of T. S. Eliot*, ed. Frank Kermode (London, 1975)

**Critical studies**
Bergonzi, B, *T. S. Eliot* (London, 1972)
Coote, S, *The Waste Land* (London, 1985)
Cox, C B & Hinchcliffe, A P (eds.) *The Waste Land: A Casebook*
(London, 1968)
Gardner, H, *The Art of T. S. Eliot* (London, 1949)
Grover Smith, C, *The Waste Land* (London, 1984)
Pinkney, A, *Women in the Poetry of T. S. Eliot: A Psychoanalytic
Approach* (London, 1984)
Southam, B C, *A Student's Guide to the Selected Poems of T. S.
Eliot* (London, 1968)
Williams, H, *T. S. Eliot: The Waste Land* (London, 1968)

**Acknowledgements**

We are grateful to the following for permission to reproduce copyright material:

Mrs Valerie Eliot & Faber and Faber Ltd for extracts from the *uncollected Writings* by T. S. Eliot and *The Waste Land: A Facsimile and Transcript* by T. S. Eliot (edited by Valerie Eliot); Faber and Faber Ltd for extracts from 'The Waste Land' from *Collected Poems 1909–1962* by T. S. Eliot.


The editors would like to thank Zachary Leader for his assistance with the style sheet.

Longman Group UK Limited
*Longman House, Burnt Mill, Harlow, Essex, CM20 2JE, England
and Associated Companies throughout the World.*

First published 1988
ISBN 0 582 00655 4

*Set in 10/12 pt Century Schoolbook, Linotron 202
Printed in Great Britain by Bell and Bain Ltd., Glasgow*